This book was brought
to you by the
Naumes Family Foundation

Hacking

The Internet

ReferencePoint
Press®

San Diego, CA

Other books in the Compact Research The Internet set:

Cyberbullying
Cyberwarfare
The Digital Divide
Online Addiction

*For a complete list of titles please visit www.referencepointpress.com.

COMPACT *Research*

Hacking

John Covaleski

The Internet

ReferencePoint
Press®

San Diego, CA

For more information, contact:
ReferencePoint Press, Inc.
PO Box 27779
San Diego, CA 92198
www.ReferencePointPress.com

Picture credits:
AP Images: 12, 17
Steve Zmina: 33–35, 48–49, 62–63, 76–77

LIBRARY OF CONGRESS CATALOGING-IN-PUBLICATION DATA

Covaleski, John.
  Hacking / by John Covaleski.
    p. cm. -- (Compact research series)
  Includes bibliographical references and index.
  ISBN 978-1-60152-268-9 (hardback) -- ISBN 1-60152-268-1 (hardback)
 1. Computer hackers--Juvenile literature. 2. Computer security--Juvenile literature. I. Title.
  HV6773.C683   2013
  364.16'8--dc23

                                                 2012014159

Contents

Foreword

As modern civilization continues to evolve, its ability to create, store, distribute, and access information expands exponentially. The explosion of information from all media continues to increase at a phenomenal rate. By 2020 some experts predict the worldwide information base will double every seventy-three days. While access to diverse sources of information and perspectives is paramount to any democratic society, information alone cannot help people gain knowledge and understanding. Information must be organized and presented clearly and succinctly in order to be understood. The challenge in the digital age becomes not the creation of information, but how best to sort, organize, enhance, and present information.

ReferencePoint Press developed the *Compact Research* series with this challenge of the information age in mind. More than any other subject area today, researching current issues can yield vast, diverse, and unqualified information that can be intimidating and overwhelming for even the most advanced and motivated researcher. The *Compact Research* series offers a compact, relevant, intelligent, and conveniently organized collection of information covering a variety of current topics ranging from illegal immigration and deforestation to diseases such as anorexia and meningitis.

The series focuses on three types of information: objective single-author narratives, opinion-based primary source quotations, and facts and statistics. The clearly written objective narratives provide context and reliable background information. Primary source quotes are carefully selected and cited, exposing the reader to differing points of view, and facts and statistics sections aid the reader in evaluating perspectives. Presenting these key types of information creates a richer, more balanced learning experience.

For better understanding and convenience, the series enhances information by organizing it into narrower topics and adding design features that make it easy for a reader to identify desired content. For example, in *Compact Research: Illegal Immigration*, a chapter covering the economic impact of illegal immigration has an objective narrative explaining the various ways the economy is impacted, a balanced section of numerous primary source quotes on the topic, followed by facts and full-color illustrations to encourage evaluation of contrasting perspectives.

The ancient Roman philosopher Lucius Annaeus Seneca wrote, "It is quality rather than quantity that matters." More than just a collection of content, the *Compact Research* series is simply committed to creating, finding, organizing, and presenting the most relevant and appropriate amount of information on a current topic in a user-friendly style that invites, intrigues, and fosters understanding.

Hacking
at a Glance

Hacking Defined

Hacking can refer to efforts to make computers and computer-based technology exceed technical limitations. More often, though, it is the act of gaining unauthorized access to computerized networks, individual computers, and other electronic devices, usually via the Internet.

Costs of Hacking

Millions of people around the world have been victimized by criminal hackers, leading to billions of dollars in financial losses.

Most Likely Victims

Small and large businesses, government agencies, and individual personal computer users are all common targets of malicious hackers.

National Security

Hackers and other cybercriminals attempt to break in to US government systems, including defense operations, thousands of times daily and sometimes succeed.

Government Response

US government defenses against hacking, first adopted after the 9/11 terrorist attacks, are continually reviewed, but there is debate about whether enough is being done.

Activist Hackers Justify their Actions

Political or social activists, known as "hacktivists," usually target government agencies and large businesses as a means of protest and to urge social change.

Stopping Hacking

The FBI and other police organizations around the world have for several years been arresting individual hackers and members of organized hacker rings on charges of stealing millions of dollars via malicious hacking.

Weak Defenses in the Business World

Businesses are finding it difficult to develop and maintain the systems required to fend off what is generally considered to be an ever-expanding threat from hackers and other cybercriminals.

Overview

> **"Simply plugging into the Internet without a properly configured firewall can get you hacked before the pizza is delivered, within 30 minutes or less."**
>
> —Stuart McClure, senior vice president and general manager of the risk and compliance unit at security software company McAfee.

> **"America's economic prosperity in the 21st century will depend on cyber security."**
>
> —Barack Obama, forty-fourth president of the United States.

Hacking is what computer users do to gain unauthorized access to or exceed their authorized access to computerized networks, individual computers, and other electronic devices—primarily by means of the Internet. The people who do the hacking usually find vulnerabilities in their targets' technologies that are unknown to the targets. These allow hackers to infiltrate the networks or devices and bypass security systems designed to ward off such attacks.

Some hackers also coax or trick computer users into disclosing restricted access information. The techniques for the trickery are called "social engineering" because the hackers use social skills to gain the confidence of users whom they dupe into providing the information. The techniques can be as simple as looking over people's shoulders to see the passwords they use to log on to their computers or networks. But they more often involve technological tricks, such as getting users to open e-mail messages or visit websites that contain software that infects their computers and gives the hackers access to the computers and their networks.

Once they gain unauthorized entry, hackers can remove or copy documents, files, and information such as business and bank account numbers from their target networks and computers or otherwise tamper with them. They also may find other security flaws to gain control of the attacked systems and computers to disrupt how they operate and to use them as launching pads to infiltrate other computers and systems.

How Serious Is the Threat from Hacking?

Hackers who illegally broke into US business and government technology systems gained access to 3.7 million documents in 2010, according to the Identity Theft Resource Center. The actual number of hacks was likely much higher, because many organizations do not disclose information about being hacked from fear it would encourage more attacks.

Hacking is so pervasive that it has helped spawn new terms, including *cybercrime* and *cyberthreat* for criminal activities related to the Internet and *cybersecurity* to describe the efforts to fight that crime.

Hacking can sometimes be surprisingly uncomplicated. In 2008 the e-mail account of Sarah Palin, who was then governor of Alaska and a candidate for vice president of the United States, was hacked by a college student. He reset Palin's e-mail account password by using information about her that he learned through an Internet Google search. The information included the governor's birth date, ZIP code, and where she met her husband. The hacker later posted an anonymous message on the Internet explaining the steps he took to pull off the hack.

> " **Hacking is so pervasive that it has helped spawn new terms, including *cybercrime* and *cyberthreat* for criminal activities related to the Internet and *cybersecurity* to describe the efforts to fight that crime.** "

The First Hackers

The first hacking of a computerized device occurred in the 1930s when a group of Polish mathematicians, led by Marian Adam Rejewski, hacked

Most high-profile hacking attacks demonstrate a sophisticated understanding of computers and cyberspace. Others are surprisingly uncomplicated, as when a college student hacked the e-mail account of Sarah Palin by gathering personal information easily accessed over the Internet.

a machine that Germany's Nazi military used for sending messages. The machine was not a computer as computers are known in the twenty-first century, but it operated with programming codes much like today's computers. The hackers determined how the machine encrypted the messages, and the discovery later helped the British military decode German messages in World War II.

Hacking as the term is now used dates back to the late 1950s, when students in the Tech Model Railroad Club at the Massachusetts Institute of Technology called themselves hackers because they were able to gain access to the internal operations of computers and then get them to do things they were not necessarily designed to do. Among their many exploits, they made paper punch cards to gain control of a mainframe computer. (Punch cards, which were the state of the art in programming computers in the 1950s, were pieces of stiff paper that contained digital information represented by the presence or absence of holes.) The computer was on the institute's campus, but the club members were authorized to use it for only limited amounts of time. The members did not do anything malicious with the computer. They hacked it because they wanted additional time to develop software programming codes with it.

Hacking Turns Malicious

Since the time of the early hackers, but more so since widespread public acceptance of the Internet in the 1990s, hacking has mushroomed into one of the most pervasive threats to global electronic communications and commerce. The Internet Crime Complaint Center, run by the FBI and other US government agencies, reported in 2011 that it was receiving and processing twenty-five thousand complaints per month. The report does not identify how many of the complaints were specifically related to hacking incidents, but it estimates that hackers cause billions of dollars of damages every year. The damage value is a combination of what the hackers steal, the costs to repair the systems they damage, and the time people and businesses lose while repairing and recovering from the hacks. Says Steven R. Chabinsky, deputy assistant director of the FBI's Cyber Division, "The cyber threat, exploiting our nation's enormous cyber vulnerability, holds the potential of being a game changer. Despite all of the advantages of computers and the Internet, if we fail to act, the cyber threat can be an existential threat—meaning it can challenge our country's very existence or significantly alter our nation's potential."[1]

Who Hacks?

There are several categories of hackers. Brian Harvey, a lecturer for the Computer Science Division at the University of California–Berkeley, believes the only true hackers are those who break into systems as a hobby or for fun. "A computer hacker is someone who lives and breathes a computer, who knows all about computers, who can get a computer to do anything," says Harvey. "Equally important, though, is the hacker's attitude."[2]

The most prominent and well publicized of all the hackers are not the hobbyists. That distinction belongs to a fast-growing element of malicious hackers who do it for money and, in many cases, illegally. These hackers are known in some circles as "black hat" hackers. They hack for

> **A hacking attack launched by North Korea incapacitated the website servers of the US Department of the Treasury, US Secret Service, Federal Trade Commission, and US Department of Transportation over a five-day period.**

Internet search engine Google was hit in 2010 by a hacking attack that sought the company's source code management system, which is the basic framework for its overall technology. The attack was unsuccessful, but accessing the code could have enabled the hackers to modify it to access the individual accounts of users of Google's e-mail service, called Gmail. Google said the hackers were from the Chinese government and wanted to access the Gmail accounts of political activists who had been crusading for human rights in China.

The damage to Google's reputation could have been serious had the attack succeeded. "Protecting a company's critical information assets like intellectual property and sensitive data has never been more important, yet challenging," says Dave DeWalt, president and chief executive officer of software security company McAfee. "A single breach or loss can cause irreparable financial damage to a company's reputation, its share price and customer confidence."[3]

Does Hacking Threaten National Security?

Governments have been mounting cyberattacks against each other since at least the start of the 2000s—and the attacks have grown bolder over time. In 2002, for instance, the US Defense Department reported that Chinese operatives stole 10 to 20 terabytes of data. An attack launched by North Korea in 2009 incapacitated the website servers of the US Department of the Treasury, US Secret Service, Federal Trade Commission, and US Department of Transportation over a five-day period. And Janet Napolitano, the director of the US Department of Homeland Security, warns that there have been instances in which hackers have come close to shutting down parts of the nation's critical infrastructure. Details on those attacks are classified information that,

After accusing the Chinese government of hacking its Gmail service to obtain information about human rights activists, Google threatened to end service in China. The company worried about its reputation, and China's many Internet users worried about losing Internet access.

if made public, could encourage more attacks on the same targets.

Mike McConnell, a former director of the National Security Agency, believes that US businesses and government agencies are destined for more and stronger cyberattacks. He argues that the need for the government to develop an Internet security system to protect America's economy from a cyberattack is as great as the need to have armed services trained to protect the country from a military attack.

Websites Under Attack

Hackers are also known to tamper with websites by, among other things, replacing home page materials with disturbing pictures and messages. Social network websites have been prime targets for such defacement attacks. Twitter was among the first victims of defacement hacks in 2009 when its home page was temporarily replaced by a black background page showing a green flag with a headline that read: "This site has been hacked by Iranian Cyber Army."[4] The hackers were believed to be Iranian Shiites (members of the Shia branch of Islam), who were upset over how Twitter was used to broadcast news about riots in Iran.

Social network sites have also attracted hackers seeking personal details about the sites' individual members. They look for clues to passwords that can be used to access personal computers, cell phones, or computer networks in the workplace.

Hacks Occurring Worldwide

While Americans hear most often about attacks in their home country, hacking is a worldwide phenomenon. Some 431 million adults in twenty-four countries experienced some type of cybercrime in 2010, according to the Norton division of security software firm Symantec.

Hacking of cell phones emerged as an issue in Great Britain in 2011 when reporters at England's *News of the World* newspaper were accused of hacking the phones of news sources and story subjects, including victims of the 2001 terrorist attacks in the United States. More than sixty of the alleged victims sued the newspaper's parent company, News Corporation, which agreed to pay millions of dollars to settle the suits.

Hacking attacks are being launched from sites around the world. Hotbeds include China and eastern Europe.

Elsewhere in England, an affiliate of weapon systems maker Raytheon reported getting 1.2 billion attacks daily on its computer network in 2011. And individual users of its network had been receiving a combined 4 million unwanted e-mail messages daily that were initiated by hackers. Says Vincent Blake, head of cybersecurity at Raytheon UK, "It's not a matter of whether something will get in your system, but more how long you will continue to have them in your system."[5]

Hacking attacks are being launched from sites around the world. Hotbeds include China and eastern Europe, where organized rings of hackers and many individual freelancers operate. These hackers break in to private business and government websites and data systems around the world with a particular interest in America. Ninety percent of technology officers at US businesses said their companies had been hacked at least once during a twelve-month period ending in early 2011, and 59 percent said they had been hacked twice, according to a survey sponsored by Juniper Networks, a developer of technology network systems. While the European hackers are reported to be common criminals with high-level technical skills, the Chinese government is believed to be supporting and organizing much of the hacking originating in that country. One attempted hack attack on some non-Chinese businesses in 2010 was traced back to servers in the headquarters of China's Public Security Bureau.

Is Hacking Ever Justifiable?

Hacktivists believe that much of what they do is justified, particularly when they hack to uncover classified government documents and publicize materials that governments would not release on their own. They also claim that by hacking a government website that is vital to a country's national interests, they show that the site is vulnerable to other attacks that could come from the country's enemies.

The hacktivist group Lulz Security in 2011 hacked the website of the CIA, temporarily crippling legitimate users' access to the site. They later hacked a US Senate website server but did not breach any data. Members of the group, which is also called LulzSec, later said their hacking was an attempt to help the government "fix their issues,"[6] such as flaws in the systems' security.

Not everyone views the actions of hacktivists as constructive. Divulging government secrets can endanger military and other personnel stationed around the world. And shutting down a government or business website can prevent customers or citizens from completing necessary transactions.

Can Hackers Be Stopped?

Businesses and government agencies are struggling in the fight against hackers. A 2011 report by the Government Accountability Office, the investigative arm of the US Congress, found that sensitive data housed by several federal agencies was at great risk of theft and compromise. Meanwhile, International Data Corporation, one of the world's best-known analysts of business technology issues, estimates that only 25 percent of all data is being properly protected.

Governments around the world are responding to the hacking epidemic by enacting laws that set stiffer penalties for convicted hackers and other cybercriminals, as well as expanding the abilities of police to investigate and arrest them. For example, in 2011 China adopted laws that criminalize the possession of hacking tools and make hacking punishable by up to seven years in prison. America led the way in cybercrime laws in 1986 when it enacted the Computer Fraud and Abuse Act, which specifically identifies unauthorized access of a computer as a criminal act and gives the FBI primary authority for investigating a big chunk of the offenses identified in the law. America adopted even tougher cyber-safety laws in the first decade of the 2000s, and in 2011 members of Congress proposed several additional bills that would give the government even more power to fight hackers.

> "The FBI has been increasing its focus on cybercrime and is developing new techniques for investigating hackers."

The FBI has been increasing its focus on cybercrime and is developing new techniques for investigating hackers. The bureau's cybercrime work recently culminated in the arrests of five members of Anonymous, LulzSec, and Operation Anti-Security in connection with the hacking of Sony and several other businesses in 2011. And in 2009 the FBI arrested one hundred people for their alleged roles in a ring that hacked banking customers' account numbers and then stole from the customers by getting them to deposit funds in a phony website. Forty-six of the suspects were convicted within two years of the arrests.

Meanwhile, Microsoft has established an international team of technologists, researchers, and investigators to fight cybercrime. It has also led consortiums of other companies and researchers in efforts to track down and stop the hackers behind some large botnets.

Hacking Fight a Cat and Mouse Game

There is no doubt that hacking poses a growing risk for computer users worldwide and that the forces fighting it are stepping up their efforts. The general sense is that the black hats will be intensifying their malicious hacking, and it is uncertain whether the white hats will be able to completely defend against these assaults. Secure Computing Corporation, an international developer of technology security systems, likens the efforts to capture and stop malicious hackers to cats trying to catch mice. The firm says, "Hackers and virus writers have become specialists, constantly developing new and innovative methods of overcoming the improvements made in today's security systems. The game of cat-and-mouse is unlikely to end any time soon."[7]

How Serious Is the Threat from Hacking?

❝One [computer] click opens the door to cybercrime.❞

—Tom Clare Sr., Director of product marketing management at technology security company Blue Coat Systems.

❝While we are more network dependent than ever before, increased interconnectivity increases the risk of theft, fraud, and abuse. No country, industry, community or individual is immune to cyber risks.❞

—Janet Napolitano, director of America's Homeland Security Department.

H acking attacks are getting bigger and costlier than ever. Hackers are stealing hundreds or thousands of dollars at a time from individuals and shutting down the operations of businesses and government agencies in attacks that cost much more money.

While individual hackers have launched crippling assaults on their own, they are increasingly working in organized groups, or rings, that make their hacking even more damaging—and more widespread. Says Martin Lee, a researcher with Symantec:

> Maverick hackers and eccentric loners have been pushed
> to the margins. Gang culture has taken root. Indeed, an
> overwhelming majority of the malware and other threats
> circulating the globe are now unleashed by well-organized

criminal gangs that are sophisticated, disciplined and frequently located in countries where they can operate with minimal interference from the authorities.[8]

Members of a ring of European hackers known as Rove Group were arrested by US law enforcement officials in November 2011. They were charged with stealing $14 million by hacking into and installing malicious software on 4 million computers in over one hundred countries, including five hundred thousand in the United States. According to the FBI, the six Estonians and one Russian identified as Rove members entered into lucrative deals in which Internet advertisers paid them for generating traffic to their websites. Using malware, the hackers forced millions of infected computers to visit the sites, resulting in millions of dollars in payments. "The international cyber threat is perhaps the most significant challenge faced by law enforcement and national security agencies today, and this case is just perhaps the tip of the Internet iceberg,"[9] says Preet Bharara, a US Attorney for the Southern District of New York, who worked on the Rove case.

The Costs of Hacking

When factoring in both the money lost to cybercrime and the cost of the time spent trying to recover from the crimes, cybercrime victims in 2010 lost an unfathomable $139 billion in the United States and $388 billion worldwide, according to software company Symantec. For businesses, costs from hacking can be enormous. For example, Sony reported more than $177 million in losses attributed to hacker attacks on two of its units—PlayStation and Sony Pictures—in 2011. This financial setback included business lost while the networks were shut down and a drop in the company's stock price. Sony also faced public image problems regarding the security of its online programs because the hackers gained access to personal information, including credit card data, from the hacked systems' 70 million users.

Cyberwarfare Threat Rising

One of the biggest rising threats is cyberwarfare hacking, in which countries target other countries to knock out their government or business systems, electrical power grids, and other pieces of infrastructure. Russia launched a cyberattack that knocked out most of the Internet connectivity in the Republic of Georgia prior to Russia's military attack on the eastern European country in 2009. The hack disrupted Georgia's defenses by blocking the Georgian people and government from sending e-mail messages outside the country. The lack of Internet and e-mail capability crippled the military's ability to share intelligence about the Russian attack and to get communications and orders from their government leaders.

> **Sony reported more than $177 million of losses attributed to hacker attacks on two of its units—Play-Station and Sony Pictures—in 2011.**

State-sponsored hacking wars have also surfaced in the Middle East. A hacking war between Israel and Saudi Arabia erupted in January 2012. Hackers in support of Israel attacked the websites of the Saudi Stock Exchange and the Abu Dhabi Securities Exchange in Saudi Arabia. The attack shut down the stock exchange and caused delays in services provided by the securities exchange. The hackers called the attacks a response to a Saudi hacker who had hacked the Tel Aviv Stock Exchange in Israel a few days earlier.

Israel has been implicated in other hacking attacks. In 2006, according to a report in the German magazine *Der Spiegel*, Israel's intelligence agency Mossad hacked into a computer that a Syrian official left unattended at a hotel. In this attack, the magazine said, Israel obtained information about a nuclear-warfare research facility in neighboring Syria. Israel subsequently bombed the facility, and Syria bulldozed the remains to hide any evidence of nuclear materials on the site. "It is not surprising to discover that Israel, a technologically advanced country under a state of siege from most of its neighbors, engages in active cyber espionage and disruption,"[10] says Richard Stiennon, founder of IT-Harvest, an Internet security research firm, and author of the security blog *ThreatChaos.com*.

Hacking Tools

Part of what makes hacking so dangerous and hard to control is that hackers steadily increase the types of tools they use for hacking. New tools can uncover and break through previously unknown vulnerabilities in computer systems, which can mean days or even weeks before system operators recognize and patch those vulnerabilities.

Hackers pull off much of their activity using software applications they design themselves or buy over the Internet. Some of the tools they use are actually designed for security professionals to protect systems from being hacked. One of these allows security analysts to probe a computer system or network for potential weaknesses that can then be patched. Using the same tool, however, a malicious hacker can also locate vulnerabilities and patches.

Other tools used by malicious hackers include devices that enable them to determine, or crack, passwords required to gain entry to computerized systems. Malicious hackers have also been known to use programs that help them gain access to information stored on computer databases. These programs enable them to log in to a database using a series of letters and numbers, which confuses the security programs.

Hackers pull off much of their activity using software applications they design themselves or buy over the Internet.

Once inside, hackers use other software tools, called sniffers, to scan and make copies of electronic data transmitted through the systems. The data can include information such as a company's business secrets and its customers' credit card numbers. Hackers are even better known for unleashing malware to cripple or gain use of the systems and computers and to change how they operate or how their functions appear to users. "Malicious hackers often think and work just like thieves, kidnappers and other organized criminals you hear about in the news every day," says Kevin Beaver, an information security consultant and author of several books that deal with defending against hackers. "The smartest ones constantly devise ways to fly under the radar and exploit even the smallest weaknesses that lead them to their target."[11]

A type of malware called Spyware lets hackers spy on the users of infected computers to see such things as the Internet sites the user visits. It can also change an infected computer's settings in ways that slow the computer's operations and otherwise interfere with functions such as the web browser used to travel the Internet.

Worms Infecting Millions of Computers

Worms, the type of malware that lets hackers gain control of infected computers, are especially threatening because of their ability to spread to other computers and give hackers' control over a vast network of computers. This network of infected computers is known as a botnet. Some botnets have consisted of as many as several million computers all infected by the same worm.

Hackers often use botnets to bombard another network or website with so much data that they shut down. These actions are known as distributed denial of service (DDOS) attacks. Russia launched such a worm-botnet attack against neighboring Estonia in 2007. The attack was part of an effort to subdue political protest after Estonians toppled a statue erected by the former Soviet Union (of which Russia was a part) to commemorate soldiers killed in World War II.

The Notorious Conficker

Among the most famous worms is Conficker, which was first detected in late 2008 and had infected an estimated 7 million government, business, and home computers in over two hundred countries by 2011. Some of the world's most knowledgeable Internet security experts and white hat hackers joined together to fight Conficker because it had the ability to launch potentially crippling attacks almost anywhere on the Internet.

> " Social engineering hacking hit a new low in 2011 when hackers loaded malware onto online computer games used by pre-school children. "

Despite its potential for causing massive disruptions, the botnet was used only to distribute a massive amount of unwanted e-mail spam messages—one of the least lethal attacks that it could have been used for. That led some investigators to suspect that Conficker's creators are a group of highly skilled computer scientists seeking to publicly demonstrate their talents in outsmarting the best security forces put together to fight hackers. The team fighting Conficker had confined the worm but not identified the hackers behind it as of early 2012.

Social Engineering

Techniques used in social engineering hacking, based on exploiting the personal weaknesses of individual computer users, are numerous. A common tactic is to trick people into downloading malicious software to their computers or to unknowingly surrender log-in and password information. On occasion, hackers have even been known to hide tiny microphones near a computer to pick up the keystrokes a user makes when logging on, an act that is called keystroke logging, or keylogging. Each keystroke emits a slightly different sound, which enables the hacker who planted the microphone to reconstruct the letters and symbols used for passwords.

Social networking sites have proved vulnerable to hacks of the profile pages of individual network members of all ages.

Social engineering hacking hit a new low in 2011 when hackers loaded malware onto online computer games used by preschool children. The toddlers, who unknowingly clicked on game links that released the malware, wound up making their computers a part of worm botnets and in some cases gave the hackers access to their parents' financial information. The games include some that let children nurture online pets or catch falling objects and others that challenge kids to spot the differences between two similar images. The hackers were looking to exploit the vulnerabilities of children too young to read.

Websites Targeted

Websites of large corporations are among hackers' preferred types of targets because those hacks give them access to information about the sites' thousands of users. In 2011 hackers obtained financial information of two hundred thousand customers of banking company Citigroup by logging on to the banking company's web page for customer service. They used phony names and passwords to log on to the site and then used a software program they developed to leapfrog from their phony accounts to the accounts of real customers. Their automatic hacking program let them repeat the leapfrogs thousands of times before Citigroup realized it was under attack and determined how to block the hacks.

TJX Companies, owner of the T.J. Maxx, Marshalls, and HomeGoods store chains, suffered one of the first truly massive website hacking attacks in 2006 when hackers stole the credit and debit card numbers of 40 million of its customers. TJX lost a reported $200 million due to the attack, which was carried out by a group of American and eastern European hackers who installed sniffer software on the company's network. The losses to TJX resulted from a combination of the costs to repair the company's technology systems and a drop in the value of its stock because of the negative publicity about the incidents.

Social Networks Under Attack

Social networking sites have proved vulnerable to hacks of the profile pages of individual network members of all ages, including teenagers. An MTV poll found that 30 percent of teenagers and young adults reported that their Facebook, Twitter, MySpace, or other Internet accounts were hacked in 2010. After a rash of hacking attacks on Twitter, which included a hack of the account of President Barack Obama in 2009, the Federal Trade Commission accused Twitter of having lax security. Twitter responded by agreeing to tighten its security system and perform security audits every two years.

Hackers also stalk social network sites for details about members, including clues about their computer passwords. In the most widely publicized incident of this type, Christopher Chaney of Jacksonville, Florida, was arrested by the FBI in 2011 and charged with hacking the e-mail and cell phone accounts of fifty celebrities and distributing files from some of the accounts. Nude photos of actress Scarlett Johansson were among the files that he allegedly hacked into and distributed. The FBI says he scanned the celebrities' social network sites to get clues for the passwords used for the hacking.

Hackers move in lockstep with everything that happens on the Internet. When people worldwide began using the Internet, hackers started showing off their talents. And as the Internet expanded into new areas, such as social networking, hackers followed. For just about anyone who goes online today, the possibility of getting hacked is very real.

Primary Source Quotes*

How Serious Is the
Threat from Hacking?

66 Ever since computing began, systems have been under threat, either by those with malicious intent, or from mistakes by well-intentioned people. As the business use of computers evolved over the years, so have the threats facing them.99

—Brian Honan, *Layered Security: Protecting Your Data in Today's Threat Landscape*. Portland, OR: Tripwire, 2011. www.tripwire.com.

Honan is a technology security consultant based in Dublin, Ireland.

66 The Internet is ubiquitous in everyday life because it shrinks the world in so many positive ways: in commerce, in academia, in entertainment, and in communications. But it is a tool, and it can be exploited by those with a little know-how and bad intentions.99

—Janice K. Fedarcyk, "Remarks as Prepared for Delivery by Assistant Director in Charge Janice K. Fedarcyk on Major Cyber Investigation," press release, FBI, November 9, 2011. www.fbi.gov.

Fedarcyk is an assistant director for the FBI at its New York office.

* Editor's Note: While the definition of a primary source can be narrowly or broadly defined, for the purposes of Compact Research, a primary source consists of: 1) results of original research presented by an organization or researcher; 2) eyewitness accounts of events, personal experience, or work experience; 3) first-person editorials offering pundits' opinions; 4) government officials presenting political plans and/or policies; 5) representatives of organizations presenting testimony or policy.

❝We are in an arms race where we're holding our own, but struggling against the inventiveness of the criminal element.❞

—Computer Security Institute, *CSI Computer Crime and Security Survey 2010/2011*. New York: Computer Security Institute, 2011. http://gocsi.com.

The Computer Security Institute of New York is an educational membership organization for information security professionals.

❝The cyber war intensifies each year, with an increasing number of attacks against payment card systems, the financial sector, and government agencies. Cyber criminals launch thousands of attacks around the world daily, costing billions of dollars.❞

—Rob Warmack, "Countering Cyber Terrorism," *Business Computing World* (blog), November 7, 2011. www.businesscomputingworld.co.uk.

Warmack is the senior director of international marketing for Tripwire, a security software development company based in Portland, Oregon.

❝Businesses will soon face an environment in which most of the code they encounter on the Web is malicious, much of it is unique or uncatalogued, and some of the worst examples are aimed directly at them.❞

—Webroot, *How to Protect Your Business from the Coming Malware Storm*, PC Magazine, 2011. http://whitepapers.pcmag.com.

Webroot is a provider of Internet services headquartered in Broomfield, Colorado.

❝To say that Web-based security attacks are on the rise would be an understatement. Consider this: In just the past three years, we've seen an eye-popping 2,000% increase in the number of DDOS attack incidents investigated on behalf of our customers.❞

—David Belson, "State of the Internet in Q3 2011: Observations on Attack Traffic," *The Akamai Blog*, January 31, 2012. https://blogs.akamai.com.

Belson is the director of market intelligence at Akamai Security Solutions, an Internet services company based in Cambridge, Massachusetts.

66 There are countless methods that hackers and cyber-criminals use to compromise the integrity, availability and confidentiality of information or services. 99

—Symantec, *Reducing the Cost and Complexity of Web Vulnerability Management*. Mountain View, CA: Symantec, 2011. www.verisign.com/ssl/ssl-information-center/ssl-resources/vulnerability-management-whitepaper.pdf.

Symantec, headquartered in Mountain View, California, develops computer security and antivirus software applications, including Norton.

66 Advances in computer technology and greater access to personal information via the Internet have created a marketplace for transnational cyber criminals to share stolen information and criminal methodologies. 99

—A.T. Smith, testimony before the US House Committee on Financial Services, Subcommittee on Financial Institutions and Consumer Credit, September 14, 2011. www.dhs.gov.

Smith is assistant director of the Secret Service in Washington, DC.

66 Financially-motivated criminals with highly-automated tools, operating from more connections in more places and exploiting new social and network vulnerabilities—any one of these factors elevates risk; taken together, they multiply it. 99

— Webroot, *How to Protect Your Business from the Coming Malware Storm*, PC Magazine, 2011. http://whitepapers.pcmag.com.

Based in Broomfield, Colorado, Webroot is a developer of Internet-based security software products.

How Serious Is the Threat from Hacking?

- In 2010 the US Secret Service arrested more than **twelve hundred** suspects for cybercrime cases that involved more than **$500 million** of fraud.

- The $388 billion that victims worldwide lost as a result of cybercrime in 2010 exceeded that year's volume of illegal trading of marijuana, cocaine, and heroin by **35 percent**, according to Symantec's Norton Cybercrime Report 2011.

- As part of its cybercrime investigations in 2010, the Secret Service examined **867 terabytes** of data, which is nearly four times the amount of data collected in the Library of Congress archives (which hold more than 151 million items, including more than 34.5 million cataloged books and other print materials and the world's largest collection of legal materials, films, maps, sheet music, and sound recordings).

- Hacking and other forms of cybercrime rank among the top four forms of **economic crimes** against businesses, according to a survey of business leaders in seventy-eight countries conducted by the consulting firm PricewaterhouseCoopers.

- During the last three months of 2011, hackers took control of an average of **209,000** computers daily in order to send spam e-mail messages, according to Internet security company Commtouch.

Older Internet Users Most at Risk

Hackers are responsible for a significant amount of Internet fraud, theft, and other online crimes. According to a report published in 2011 by the Internet Crime Working Group, the two largest groups reporting Internet crimes in 2010 were between the ages of 40 and 59. The group that appeared to have the lowest risk of becoming a victim of Internet crime was the under-20 category. The report also notes that the most dramatic rise in complaints of Internet crime over the past 10 years has taken place in the 60-and-older category.

Cybercrime Victims by Age

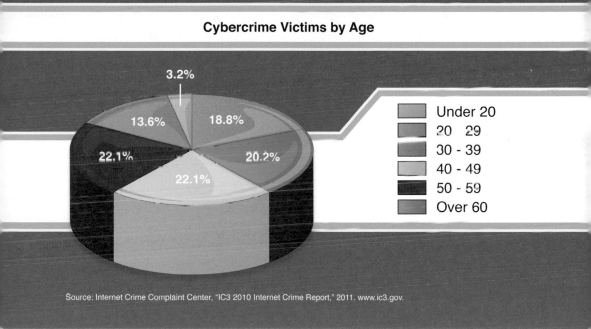

Under 20	
20 29	
30 - 39	
40 - 49	
50 - 59	
Over 60	

3.2%
13.6%
18.8%
22.1%
20.2%
22.1%

Source: Internet Crime Complaint Center, "IC3 2010 Internet Crime Report," 2011. www.ic3.gov.

- The proportion of personal accounts on social network websites that became infected by malware increased from **13 percent** in 2010 to 18 percent in 2011, according security services firm Webroot.

- Malware attacks were the most common form of cybercrime inflicted on American businesses in the twelve-month period ending on June 30, 2010, accounting for **67.1 percent** of all the business cybercrime reported in a survey by the FBI and the Computer Security Institute.

Cybercrime Ranks High Among Crimes of Fraud

Cybercrime has emerged as one of the top forms of fraud experienced by business worldwide, according to a PricewaterhouseCoopers survey published in 2011. Nearly one in four respondents who experienced some form of financial fraud in 2011 said they had suffered one or more cybercrime incidents during that period. The researchers noted in their findings that the number who reported experiencing cybercrime in previous economic crime surveys was so low that it was considered statistically insignificant—a marked difference from the results of this more recent survey.

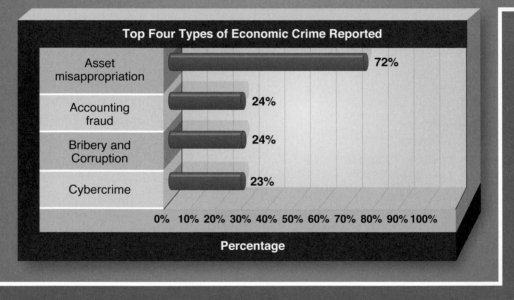

Top Four Types of Economic Crime Reported

Type	Percentage
Asset misappropriation	72%
Accounting fraud	24%
Bribery and Corruption	24%
Cybercrime	23%

0% 10% 20% 30% 40% 50% 60% 70% 80% 90% 100%

Percentage

Source: PricewaterhouseCoopers, "Cybercrime: Protecting Against the Growing Threat Global Economic Crime Survey," November 2011. www.pwc.com.

- American businesses whose technology systems were hacked or otherwise breached in 2009 lost an average of **$6.76 million** as a result of the break-ins, according to the Michigan-based research firm Ponemon Institute.

- The business consulting firm Boston Consulting Group estimates that the dollar value of Internet-based business done by countries with large economies will reach **$4.2 trillion** in 2016, nearly double the size it was in 2010.

Potential Targets for Hackers Proliferate

The proliferation of electronic devices with Internet and network connections has created a vast number of potential targets for hackers. The number of information technology (IT) devices, including computers and cell phones, that are connected to networks and the Internet is expected to grow to 50 billion in 2020 from less than 1 billion in 2003.

Projected Growth in Number of IT Devices Connected to Networks and the Internet, 2003–2020

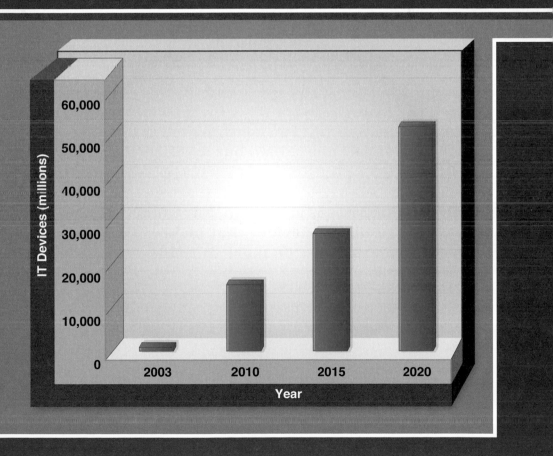

Source: Cisco Systems, as cited by the Office of the National Counterintelligence Executive, "Foreign Spies Stealing U.S. Economic Secrets in Cyberspace, Report to Congress on Foreign Economic Collection and Industrial Espionage 2009–2011." October 2011.

Does Hacking Threaten National Security?

66Stopping terrorists is the number one priority. But down the road, the cyber threat will be the number one threat to the country. I do not think today it is necessarily [the] number one threat, but it will be tomorrow.99

—Robert Mueller III, director of the FBI.

66The United States is reliant on, but cannot secure, the networks of digital devices that make up cyberspace. As a nation, we must do more to reduce risk, and we must do it soon.99

—Commission on Cybersecurity for the 44th Presidency, a group established in 2007 to advise then-candidate Barack Obama on cybersecurity issues.

Fears abound about the possibility for hackers to launch a major cyberattack that cripples the United States in ways not felt since the start of World War II, when the Japanese attacked the US Naval Fleet in Pearl Harbor, Hawaii. "There is a strong likelihood that the next Pearl Harbor that we confront could very well be a cyber-attack that cripples our power systems, our grid, our security systems, our financial systems, our governmental systems. This is a real possibility in today's world,"[12] says Leon Panetta, US secretary of defense and a former director of the CIA.

The United States Presents a Big Target

Computers and servers in the United States are the most aggressively targeted information systems in the world, with hacking attacks increasing in severity, frequency, and sophistication each year, says the Federal Emergency Management Agency. Groups in China have launched numerous cyberattacks on the United States. Symantec reports that Chinese groups hacked forty-eight US defense contractors in 2011.

A hacking attack launched by North Korea against the United States incapacitated the website servers of the Treasury Department, Secret Service, Federal Trade Commission, and the US Department of Transportation over a five-day period in July 2009. The Koreans used a botnet that consisted of forty thousand zombie computers pinging the servers with as many as 1 million requests for information per second in a DDOS attack. The hackers also struck the White House computer systems, causing a slowdown in a server that covered parts of Asia. Servers for the New York Stock Exchange, the NASDAQ Stock Market, and the *Washington Post* newspaper were also hit in the hacking barrage.

> " Computers and servers in the United States are the most aggressively targeted information systems in the world, with hacking attacks increasing in severity, frequency, and sophistication each year. "

The government of China has also established itself as a significant cyberthreat to US businesses and government agencies. Mike McConnell, a former director of the National Security Agency; Michael Chertoff, a former secretary of the Department of Homeland Security; and William Lynn, a former deputy secretary of defense, coauthored an opinion article in the *Wall Street Journal* that accuses China of having a national policy of cyber espionage against the United States. They further say, "The Chinese are the world's most active and persistent practitioners of cyber espionage today."[13]

The ultimate aim of cyber espionage is to obtain valuable government and corporate secrets. China views economic espionage as an "essential tool in achieving national security and economic prosperity,"[14] says a 2011 report from the Office of the National Counterintelligence Executive, which gathers information from law enforcement and intelligence collection bodies that include the National Security Agency and the CIA.

Cyberterrorists

There are growing concerns that terrorists from the Middle East will aim cyberattacks at America. "Terrorists have shown interest in pursuing hacking skills," warns FBI director Robert Mueller III. "And they may seek to train their own recruits or hire outsiders, with an eye toward pursuing cyberattacks. These adaptations of the terrorist threat make the FBI's counter-terrorism mission that much more difficult and challenging."[15]

Mueller is particularly concerned about the potential cyberthreat from al Qaeda, which launched the 2001 terrorist attacks on the United States. He says the group's use of the Internet is evolving, noting that it uses online chat rooms and services, including Twitter, to recruit followers and encourage terrorism.

Chinese Military Suspected of Hacking US Space Satellites

Hackers believed to be from the Chinese military interfered with two US government satellites four times in 2007 and 2008, according to a 2011 report from the US-China Economic and Security Review Commission, an agency that monitors dealings between the two countries. The commission does not provide details on how China hacked the satellites, which are used for observing climate conditions. However, it warns that the actions may be part of China's effort to broaden its cyberwarfare capabilities. The commission's report notes:

> China's military strategy envisions the use of computer network exploitation and attack against adversaries, including the United States. These efforts are likely to focus on operational systems, such as command, control, communications, computers, intelligence, surveillance, and reconnaissance assets. This could critically disrupt the U.S. military's ability to deploy and operate during a military contingency.[16]

Aurora Attack

The search engine company Google says that the Chinese have repeatedly tried to hack its operations to prevent it from doing business in their country. Some of the Google attacks were part of Operation Aurora, a large-scale hacking attack in 2009 that also hit other information technology companies, including Adobe Systems, Juniper Networks, and Cisco Systems. The hackers were trying to obtain access to source code management systems, which provide a framework for their overall technologies. Access to those systems would have enabled the hackers to make changes that would have left customers vulnerable to hacking attacks.

The Aurora hackers gained initial access to the networks by sending the companies' workers e-mail messages that appeared friendly but contained links to a website hosted in Taiwan. The site, in turn, released malware that attacked vulnerabilities in the Internet Explorer software on the workers' computers, which gave the hackers network access. Microsoft, the maker of Internet Explorer, later corrected those vulnerabilities. McAfee, a security software company that investigated the attacks, said the hackers had indeed accessed the source code of some companies, but none of the companies reported any major damage.

> " There are growing concerns that terrorists from the Middle East will aim cyberattacks at America. "

The attack alerted the technology security field that private businesses are vulnerable to the same devastating level of hacking attacks that have been focused on the US government. "We have never ever, outside of the defense industry, seen commercial industrial companies come under that level of sophisticated attack," says Dmitri Alperovitch, vice president of threat research for McAfee. "It's totally changing the threat model."[17]

Government Intervenes in Attacks on Businesses

The ability of hackers to break into the operations of private businesses, particularly banks and other financial services companies, is considered a national security concern. Such attacks, or even the threat of them, can

> The ability of hackers to break into the operations of private businesses, particularly banks and other financial services companies is considered a national security concern.

hurt economic activity. "The biggest scare in cyberspace will be more emotional and psychological than it will be actual," says Dale Meyerrose, a former chief information officer for the Director of National Intelligence. "People will lose trust in their ability to do banking online and their ability to buy things online and their ability to use an ATM."[18]

The demonstrated potential for hackers to launch cyberattacks on individual businesses prompted the Obama administration to adopt cybersecurity measures specifically for businesses and industries in 2011. Among the measures is one that requires businesses to report technology system breaches to the US Securities and Exchange Commission (SEC) and another that requires the National Security Agency, an investigative unit of the US Department of Defense, to share intelligence on foreign hackers with banks. The FBI also began warning banks about hacking threats. Says Shawn Henry, executive assistant director of the FBI's Criminal, Cyber, Response, and Services Branch, "We know adversaries have full unfettered access to certain networks. Once there, they have the ability to destroy data. We see that as a credible threat to all sectors, but specifically the financial services sector."[19]

Congress Proposes Cybersecurity Measures

The US House of Representatives and US Senate have reviewed many proposed laws designed to guard against massive cybersecurity threats. Among them, the Cybersecurity Act of 2012 is aimed at protecting key infrastructure areas, such as the power grid and financial markets. Either could be targeted by a cyberattack designed to cripple the country overall. The bill would create a government agency responsible for setting cybersecurity standards for key infrastructure areas and require businesses in those areas to meet the standards. It would also establish programs under which those businesses would provide the government information about cybersecurity matters. Congress is also considering the Cyber Intelligence Sharing and Protection Act. This law would allow Internet service providers and Internet companies to monitor and collect any information on users that they think might pose a threat to their systems and to share that information with government investigators.

Government Response Lacking

Some former high-ranking government officials say that the government is not reacting forcefully enough to the cyberthreat. According to Mike McConnell, director of the National Security Agency under President Bill Clinton and director of the Director of National Intelligence under President George W. Bush, "The United States is fighting a cyber-war today, and we are losing. As the most wired nation on Earth, we offer the most targets of significance, yet our cyber-defenses are woefully lacking."[20]

Richard A. Clarke, who held key national security positions in the administrations of presidents Bill Clinton, Ronald Reagan, George H.W. Bush, and George W. Bush, warns that the country needs to broaden its approach to cybersecurity. "In the daily guerrilla cyber war with China, our government is engaged in defending only its own networks. It is failing in its responsibility to protect the rest of America from Chinese cyber-attack,"[21] says Clarke, now a business consultant and lecturer at Harvard University's John F. Kennedy School of Government.

Privacy Concerns

Some say the government is not doing enough to protect against cyberattacks; others worry the government is doing too much. Some of the efforts to safeguard the country from cyberwarfare raise concerns about infringements on individual citizens' rights. The Electronic Privacy Information Center, a public interest research organization, warns that the information sharing that the Cybersecurity Act and the Cyber Intelligence Sharing and Protection Act would allow could infringe on citizens' rights to privacy. "Since we are talking about privately owned and operated networks that carry personal communications, any sharing of information must be carefully controlled,"[22] says Gregory Nojeim, a project director at the nonprofit public policy group Center for Democracy & Technology.

Nojeim warns that the amount and type of information that is collected or shared needs to be limited and needs to be used only for cybersecurity efforts. The concern is that police could use information gathered about individual citizens to investigate those citizens for alleged crimes not related to cybersecurity, something that would violate citizens' privacy. In February 2012 a subcommittee of the US House Committee on Homeland Security proposed a bill that would create a quasi-governmental organization to oversee information sharing and would define what information can be shared. Nojeim thinks this bill is a good step toward protecting the privacy of US citizens.

> **Some former high-ranking government officials say that the government is not reacting forcefully enough to the cyberthreat.**

Meanwhile, the SEC expects some businesses to resist complying with its guidelines for reporting on technology system breaches, because making such information public could be seen as harmful to their reputations. Says Jody Westby, chief executive officer of Global Cyber Risk, a consulting firm to large businesses, "Companies involved in breaches are very reluctant to reveal what happened, and much less tell the SEC what happened. Why? Because of a fear of reputational damage."[23]

However, many technology security specialists welcome the government's efforts to establish a national defense system against cyberattacks. "Governments can make targets harder to attack, and they can use intelligence capabilities to gain advance knowledge of when attacks may take place,"[24] says one of the world's largest security software companies, Symantec.

Risk and Response

The threat that hackers pose for US government and businesses shows no signs of slowing. The number of attempts to hack into government computers and data increased by a factor of six or more between 2006 and 2010, according to a report by the Government Accountability Office. The report also warns, "Weaknesses in information security policies and practices at 24 major federal agencies continue to place the confidentiality, integrity and availability of sensitive information and information systems at risk."[25]

While there is no doubt that the threat hacking poses to America is dramatic and growing, there is no consensus on how the country should respond. Whatever responses are finally crafted is unlikely to satisfy individuals, agencies, and corporations on all sides of the issue.

Primary Source Quotes*

Does Hacking Threaten National Security?

66 It is unlikely that there will ever be a true cyberwar.99

—Peter Sommer and Ian Brown, *Reducing Systemic Cybersecurity Risk*, OECD/IFP Project on Future Global Shocks, January 14, 2011. www.oecd.org.

Sommer is with the Information Systems and Innovation Group of the London School of Economics; Brown is with the Oxford Internet Institute of Oxford University.

66 Sensitive information is routinely stolen from both government and private sector networks, undermining confidence in our information systems, the information collection and sharing process, and the information these systems contain. Recognizing the serious nature of this challenge, the President made cybersecurity an administration priority upon taking office.99

—Richard W. Downing, testimony before the US House of Representatives subcommittee on Crime, Terrorism, and National Security, November 15, 2011. www.cybercrime.gov.

Downing is deputy chief of the US Department of Justice's Computer Crime & Intellectual Property Section.

* Editor's Note: While the definition of a primary source can be narrowly or broadly defined, for the purposes of Compact Research, a primary source consists of: 1) results of original research presented by an organization or researcher; 2) eyewitness accounts of events, personal experience, or work experience; 3) first-person editorials offering pundits' opinions; 4) government officials presenting political plans and/or policies; 5) representatives of organizations presenting testimony or policy.

> **The cybersecurity debate is stuck. . . . We need new concepts and new strategies if we are to reduce the risks in cyberspace to the United States.**

—Commission on Cybersecurity for the 44th Presidency, *Cybersecurity Two Years Later*. Washington, DC: Center for Strategic and International Studies, 2011.

The Commission on Cybersecurity for the 44th Presidency was established in 2007 to advise then-candidate Barack Obama on cybersecurity issues.

> **Senior U.S. officials know well that the government of China is systematically attacking the computer networks of the U.S. government and American corporations. Beijing is successfully stealing research and development, software source code, manufacturing know-how and government plans.**

—Richard A. Clarke, "China's Cyberassault on America," *Wall Street Journal*, June 15, 2010. http://online.wsj.com.

Clarke is a consultant and lecturer at Harvard University's John F. Kennedy School of Government; he held key national security positions in the administrations of Presidents Bill Clinton, Ronald Reagan, and George H.W. Bush.

> **Securing cyberspace is an absolute imperative.**

—Jeffrey Carr, *Inside Cyber Warfare*. Sebastopol, CA: O'Reilly Media, 2010.

Carr is a consultant to governments on information security matters, an author, and a public speaker; he lives in Seattle, Washington.

> **A number of governments have cybersecurity programs and some have announced they are developing cyber-weapons. Still, we're unprepared for cyberwar consequences.**

—Dan Blum, "Proposing an International Cyberweapons Control Protocol," *Gartner Blog Network*, February 20, 2012. http://blogs.gartner.com.

Blum is a senior vice president and principal analyst with Gartner, a technology industry research firm.

66 China and Russia are of particular concern. Entities within these countries are responsible for extensive illicit intrusions into US computer networks and theft of US intellectual property. 99

—James R. Clapper, testimony before the US House of Representatives' Permanent Select Committee on Intelligence, February 2, 2012. http://intelligence.house.gov.

Clapper is America's director of National Intelligence.

66 Cyber warfare is attractive to adversaries because it poses a significant threat at a low cost. An adversary does not need an expensive weapons program to conduct damaging attacks; a handful of programmers could cripple an entire information system. 99

—Government Accountability Office, *Defense Department Cyber Efforts: DOD Faces Challenges in Its Cyber Activities.* Washington, DC: Government Accountability Office, July 2011.

The Government Accountability Office is the investigative arm of the US Congress.

66 There is a huge future threat, and there is a considerable current threat. And that's just the reality that we all face. 99

—Robert Gates, "Remarks by Secretary Gates at the Wall Street Journal CEO Council 2010 Meeting," news transcript, US Department of Defense, November 16, 2010. www.defense.gov.

Gates served as America's secretary of defense from 2006 until 2011 and previously worked for the CIA and the National Security Council.

Facts and Illustrations

Does Hacking Threaten National Security?

- America's Defense Department estimates that its computers and networks are probed by hackers and other unwanted intruders about **6 million** times every day. Many of the probes are attempts to gain unauthorized access to the department.

- The **Chinese** are the world's most active and persistent perpetrators of economic espionage, which mainly involves cyberattacks on businesses, according to a 2011 report by the Office of the National Counterintelligence Executive, which is part of America's Director of National Intelligence operations.

- In 2011 the Office of the National Counterintelligence Executive identified **hacktivists** as among the major threats to American security.

- **Russia's intelligence services** were involved in several efforts in 2011 to gather economic information and technology from American organizations, according to the Office of the National Counterintelligence Executive.

- **Fifty-seven percent** of the world's leading's authorities on global security believe that nations around the world are in a "cyber arms race" to develop stronger capabilities to mount and defend against cyberattacks, according to a 2012 survey by security software company McAfee and Security & Defence Agenda, a research organization in Belgium.

Hacking Incidents Skyrocket at Government Agencies

Hacking of government computer systems has been steadily rising, according to statistics compiled by the US Computer Emergency Readiness Team (US-CERT). US-CERT is a coalition of government agencies and private groups involved in crafting a government response to a possible computer system emergency. According to the group's 2011 report, incidents of hacking and attempted hacking of federal government computers rose dramatically from about 5,000 in 2006 to more than 40,000 in 2010.

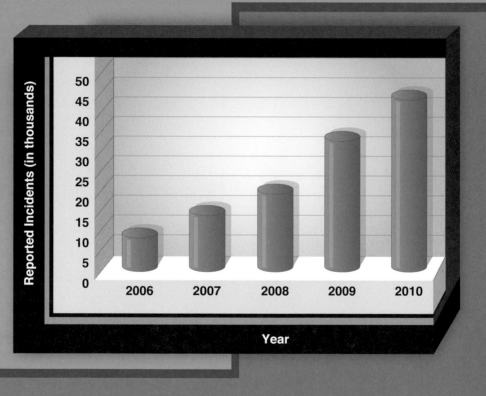

Source: United States Government Accountability Office, "Information Security Weaknesses Continue Amid New Federal Efforts to Implement Requirements," October 2011. www.gao.gov.

• Cyberdefense is more important than having missile defense systems, according to **36 percent** of the security experts who responded to the McAfee and Security & Defence Agenda survey.

Confidence in Governments' Cyberdefense Capability Is Maxed

Information technology (IT) executives in the critical civilian infrastructure areas of energy, oil and gas, and water have mixed views on whether their governments can prevent or deter cyberattacks. According to a 2011 survey conducted by security software company McAfee, confidence is highest in Japan, which has increased its focus on regulation and audits. Confidence was lowest in Brazil. IT executives in the United States express a moderate level of confidence in the government's ability to prevent or deter cyberattacks. Overall, the report states, vulnerabilities are growing but preparation and response protocols are not keeping pace.

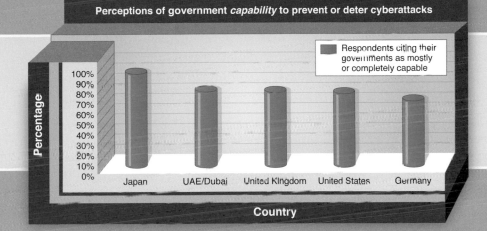

Perceptions of government *capability* to prevent or deter cyberattacks

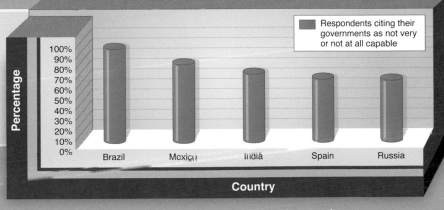

Perceptions of government *incapability* to prevent or deter cyberattacks

Source: McAfee, "In the Dark: Crucial Industries Confront Cyberattacks," 2011, p. 21. www.mcafee.com.

- The quality of America's **cyberwarfare readiness** ranks below that of several smaller countries, including Israel, Sweden, and Finland, according to the McAfee and Security & Defence Agenda survey.

- From July 1, 2010, through June 30, 2011, the Homeland Security Department estimated that it prevented **$1.5 billion** in losses through its cybercrime investigations.

- In 2010, despite a growing federal budget deficit, the Defense Department committed **$500 million** to a project that is researching development of more effective ways to encrypt data.

- American companies in critical infrastructure areas that include public utilities and finance would have to increase their spending on technology security by a factor of nine to guarantee they are protected from a **crippling cyberattack**, according to a study by the Ponemon Institute and the government research unit of the Bloomberg news organization.

- The number of security incidents, including hacking, reported by US government agencies increased by **650 percent** between 2006 and 2011, according to the Government Accountability Office.

Is Hacking Justifiable?

> **LulzSec is a timely wake-up call to better security if you are still asleep at the wheel. Your customers' data is important—both to them and to you.**
>
> —Paul Ducklin, head of technology for the Asia-Pacific business unit of security software company Sophos.

> **One man's hacktivists is another man's cyber terrorists.**
>
> —Kevin G. Coleman, a senior fellow with the Technolytics Institute, which advises on cybersecurity and other technology issues.

George Hotz, a hacker from Glen Rock, New Jersey, decided his PlayStation 3 (PS3) video game system needed improvement in 2009. So he hacked into the inner workings of his console, made some changes, and then posted them on his personal website for all to see. Hotz had enabled his game system to do things the manufacturer had never intended. And thanks to Hotz's web postings, other PS3 owners could do the same. Hotz saw his achievement as a victory for consumers everywhere, sort of a David versus Goliath scenario. "They'll never understand people like us," Hotz later said of Sony, which manufactures the PS3. "They are scared, as they rightfully should be. We built your PS3. We built this world. We are not mindless consumers."[26]

Sony saw things differently. The company sued Hotz for violating copyright laws that prohibit people from publicly distributing information or devices designed to alter copyrighted software, such as what was inside the PS3. The two sides settled out of court in 2011.

This was not the first time Hotz had placed himself in the role of the consumer's David. In 2007, at the age of seventeen, he hacked into an Apple iPhone shortly after the new devices went on sale. Apple then had an exclusive deal with AT&T to provide the data and communications network for its iPhones. Hotz found a way to connect the iPhone to other carriers and shared his discovery and methods online. Apple took no action against Hotz, but it did modify later models to prevent the changes the hacker had devised.

Public Service or Public Menace?

The Hotz story illustrates one of the key issues in the debate over hacking: Do hackers perform a public service by finding and publicizing flaws (or improvements) in products, popular websites, government agency servers, personal information storage methods, and other online tools? Or do they violate privacy, trespass on corporate property, and endanger private individuals and government operations by their actions?

In the last few years, groups of hacktivists have broken into government and corporate websites. Members of these groups say they use their talents to expose lies, corruption, and other dishonest practices, as well as flawed technologies. The hacktivists are small in number, accounting for just 2 percent of the total number of data breaches that occurred worldwide in 2011, according to a 2012 report by Verizon Communications and government investigators in the United States, Australia, Ireland, and Netherlands. The report notes, however, that hacktivists stole more than 100 million individual records—which exceeds the number of records stolen by cybercriminals whose goal was financial gain.

> **Members of these groups say they use their talents to expose lies, corruption, and other dishonest practices, as well as flawed technologies.**

Hacktivists established themselves as menaces in 2011, according to the report. It notes that businesses, in particular, consider hacktivism a bigger threat than hacking done purely for theft. At least with thieves, the intent is clear. With hacktivists, businesses often do not understand their reasons or their intentions. "Enemies are even scarier when you can't predict their behavior,"[27] the report says.

Two of the best-known hacktivist groups, LulzSec and Anonymous, teamed up in June 2011 to launch a series of attacks on businesses and governments. Their stated intention was to make public classified information that they believe should not be kept secret. They called their effort Operation Anti-Security, or AntiSec, and described themselves as engaging in a war. In an online letter to the general public, LulzSec said, "The government and White Hat security terrorists across the world continue to dominate and control our Internet ocean. Sitting pretty on cargo bays full of corrupt booty, they think it's acceptable to condition and enslave all vessels in sight. Our Lulz Lizard battle fleet is now declaring immediate and unremitting war on the freedom-snatching moderators of 2011."[28]

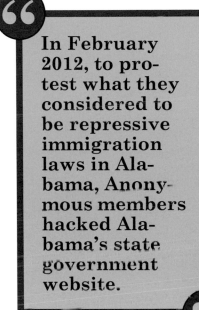

In February 2012, to protest what they considered to be repressive immigration laws in Alabama, Anonymous members hacked Alabama's state government website.

Later in the year members of Anonymous launched an attack against law enforcement offices in several states to protest hacker arrests. As part of the assault, the hackers stole data from seventy-six websites in eleven states, most of it from sheriffs' departments in Arkansas, Kansas, Louisiana, Mississippi, and Missouri.

Anonymous Versus Syria

Foreign governments have also felt the wrath of hacktivists. Anonymous kicked off a battle with Syria in 2011 to protest that government's crushing attacks on rebels seeking an end to dictatorship. As part of that protest Anonymous hacked into and defaced several Syrian government websites. The attack spurred a counterattack by Syrian government sympathizers, who hacked and defaced the websites of several large American universities, including Harvard and the University of California–Los Angeles. The sympathizers may have chosen large universities in order to gain greater public notice of their actions. They posted a picture of Assad on the sites with a message that said, "We love our country and we love our president."[29]

Hacktivist efforts continued in February 2012 when members of Anonymous hacked into e-mail servers in the office of Syrian president Bashar al-Assad. Anonymous obtained hundreds of e-mail messages from the in-boxes of Assad and his staff and distributed them over the Internet. Materials that were leaked to the public included instructions that a government advisor gave Assad to prepare him for a television interview with Barbara Walters of ABC News in December 2011. The leaked e-mails showed that his advisors had suggested answers aimed at finding favor with American television viewers. For instance, Assad admitted in the interview that he made mistakes in handling the rebels because he was told that Americans will forgive people who admit mistakes. He also tried to portray himself as a hero who was under attack by the rebels because he was told that Americans admire heroism.

Social Protest Hackings

In February 2012, to protest what they considered to be repressive immigration laws in Alabama, Anonymous members hacked Alabama's state government website. They gained access to the personal records of forty-six thousand state residents and later released the records of several hundred online. Anonymous posted an online message saying that its actions were a response to Alabama's disregard for immigrants.

In 2011 the Alabama legislature enacted what was considered one the nation's harshest immigration laws. Among other things, the law makes it a criminal offense to give a ride to immigrants who do not have proper government documents regarding their immigration status. It also requires public schools to check students' immigration status and instructs police to check the immigration status of anyone they stop if they suspect the person of being in the United States illegally.

Who Are the Hacktivists?

Anonymous is believed to have hundreds of members in the United States and around the world. The members meet and share ideas, including thoughts on who should be hacked and why, via e-mail or on Internet websites. LulzSec, which is affiliated with Anonymous, is believed to have fewer members, most of whom are from the United States and Great Britain. Several other less-known hacktivist organizations that are affiliated with Anonymous include AntiSec and a group called Internet Feds.

Anonymous has primarily been known for hacking in support of their members' opinions regarding needs for social, political, or economic changes. LulzSec members are known to hack largely to make fun of their targets' weak security.

Highlighting Security Flaws

One of the justifications that hacktivists give for their actions is that they vividly demonstrate potentially harmful security flaws in hacked websites, servers, and networks. Highlighting such flaws, they contend, provides system operators with the opportunity to take steps to correct the shortfalls. They also see themselves as watching out for common citizens who are unaware of such flaws in the government or business systems that they may use.

In an open letter to Internet users in 2011, members of LulzSec claimed credit for hacking the site of the social network Facebook. They warned users about weak security on social networking and other popular Internet sites and programs. The group wrote:

> Do you feel safe with your Facebook accounts, your Google Mail accounts, and your Skype accounts? What makes you think a hacker isn't silently sitting inside all of these right now, sniping out individual people, or perhaps selling them off? You are a peon to these people, a toy, a string of characters with a value. This is what you should be fearful of, not us releasing things publicly, but the fact that someone hasn't released something publicly.[30]

Likewise, a hacktivist group called Goatse Security hacked AT&T in 2010 to get access to the accounts of 114,000 users of its iPad 3G cell phone network. They claimed they did it as a service to AT&T customers, by showing the system's vulnerabilities. AT&T subsequently patched the system hole the Goatse group hacked through and apologized to its iPad customers for the breach.

WikiLeaks

WikiLeaks is an online news-gathering organization famous for obtaining classified documents from the US Department of State and the US military and distributing them to newspapers and other news outlets. It gained a large and vocal following among political activists and hacktivists after it released those documents in 2010. Those who believe that government secrecy threatens the welfare of the country and the world have applauded the actions of WikiLeaks, which is often viewed as a hacktivist organization. Peter Ludlow, a professor of philosophy at Northwestern University, argues that WikiLeaks and its founder, Julian Assange, should be considered heroes for publicizing the documents. He calls WikiLeaks "the product of decades of collaborative work by people engaged in applying computer hacking to political causes, in particular, to the principle that information-hoarding is evil."[31]

Members of Anonymous also came to the defense of WikiLeaks by launching hacking attacks on the websites of credit card companies MasterCard and Visa in the summer of 2011. The two companies had expressed their opposition to WikiLeaks' actions by ceasing the handling of credit card payments made on the WikiLeaks site.

Foreign governments have also felt the wrath of hacktivists.

The US government does not consider WikiLeaks' actions to be heroic or justifiable. The US Army arrested Private First Class Bradley Manning, the soldier accused of stealing the documents and giving them to Assange. His court martial is set for September 21, 2012. The government contends that the leaked documents jeopardized the war effort in Afghanistan and put soldiers there at greater risk. Says Michael Mullen, chair of the Joint Chiefs of Staff, "Mr. Assange can say whatever he likes about the greater good he thinks he and his sources are doing, but the truth is they might already have on their hands the blood of some young soldier, or that of an Afghan family."[32]

News Media Phone Hacking

The *News of the World* newspaper in London was forced to shut down in 2011 amid an investigation into allegations that its reporters repeatedly hacked cell phones to get information for stories. But one of the paper's former editors, Paul McMullan, says the reporters' hacking was part of their journalistic mission to report vital information. "If you want a free democracy and open society, you have to be there to catch people," he says. "You cannot just ask them, you have to be cleverer and have to catch them."[33] However, Paul Connolly, an editor with another British newspaper, the *Telegraph*, argues that the *News of World*'s actions were not justified. "It is simply illegal to hack into phones,"[34] he says.

During the investigation, hundreds of allegations surfaced that *News of the World* reporters hacked the cell phones of some of Britain's leading political figures, celebrities, and even crime victims. Police estimated that the paper's reporters hacked the phones of about eight

> " The *News of the World* newspaper in London was forced to shut down in 2011 amid an investigation into allegations that its reporters repeatedly hacked cell phones. "

hundred people. The reporters were accused of using fraudulent personal identification numbers to hack into the victims' voice mail messages. Cell phone companies in England subsequently implemented security procedures to protect against the type of hacking perpetrated by the *News of the World* reporters.

The Evolving World of Hackers

Hacking has experienced an unusual evolution. What began as an intellectual challenge later became the province of petty thieves, then organized criminal rings, and eventually a tool of warfare between nations. "Then hackers turned to politics, and political activists turned to hacking," writes Eric Sterner, a fellow at the George C. Marshall Institute. "Unfortunately, a marriage that began as a partnership aimed at protest is now often dealing in aggression. Rather than expressing political opinions, organizing for political action or even engaging in the kind of online demonstrations that have often earned admiring—if not always positive—attention, some hacktivists have turned to outright belligerence."[35] Hackers of various stripes cite many reasons for their actions. Whether those actions can be justified remains a topic for debate in the years ahead.

Is Hacking Justifiable?

Primary Source Quotes

66 For hacktivists, 2011 marked a turning point in which they morphed from cutting-edge cyber street artists eager to stick it to the powerful into a national security threat, at least in the eyes of a growing number of security professionals. This characterization may not be fair, or even accurate, but the perception is understandable. 99

Eric Sterner, "Hacktivists' Evolution Changes Cyber Security Threat Environment," *World Politics Review*, April 23, 2012.

Eric Sterner is a fellow at the George C. Marshall Institute, which assesses issues in science and technology and their impact on public policy.

66 Nobody is truly causing the Internet to slip one way or the other; it's an inevitable outcome for us humans. We've been entertaining you 1000 times with 140 characters or less, and we'll continue creating things that are exciting and new until we're brought to justice, which we might well be. 99

—LulzSec, "LulzSec—1000th Tweet Statement," press release, Pastebin.com, June 17, 2011. http://pastebin.com.

LulzSec is a hacktivist group.

* Editor's Note: While the definition of a primary source can be narrowly or broadly defined, for the purposes of Compact Research, a primary source consists of: 1) results of original research presented by an organization or researcher; 2) eyewitness accounts of events, personal experience, or work experience; 3) first-person editorials offering pundits' opinions; 4) government officials presenting political plans and/or policies; 5) representatives of organizations presenting testimony or policy.

66 Hackers have truly a mindset of how to approach a problem. So, sort of like you can have a criminal plumber or a good plumber, you can have a criminal hacker or a bad hacker, so we call them computer criminals. But the hacking mindset [is] how to make technology do things it was never intended to do. . . . How does the technology really work, not how do you think it works. 99

—Jeff Moss, "Jeff Moss on Hackers, Cyber Security Threats," video, *PBS NewsHour*, August, aired 10, 2010. www.pbs.org.

Moss is an ethical hacker who founded and now organizes Black Hat and DEF CON, annual conventions attended by ethical and unethical hackers from around the world.

66 Just as Sherlock Holmes's work was about solving puzzles as much as it was about catching criminals, and miscreants, my hacking, too, was always concerned in some way with unraveling mysteries and meeting challenges. 99

—Kevin Mitnick, *Ghost in the Wires: My Adventures as the World's Most Wanted Hacker*. New York: Little, Brown, 2011.

Mitnick is a security consultant and author who was convicted twice, in 1988 and 1995, of crimes related to hacking government and business organizations and served time in prison.

66 Exploring security on your devices is cool, hacking into someone else's server and stealing databases of user info is not cool. 99

—George Hotz, "Recent News," *GeoHot Got Sued* (blog), April 20, 2011. http://geohotgotsued.blogspot.com.

Hotz is a security consultant who is better known as a hacker and goes by the Internet name GeoHot.

> 66 Many hackers don't necessarily want to steal your information or crash your systems. They often just want to prove to themselves and their buddies that they can break in. This likely creates a warm fuzzy feeling that makes them feel like they're contributing to society somehow. 99

—Kevin Beaver, *Hacking for Dummies*, 3rd ed. Hoboken, NJ: Wiley, 2010.

Beaver is an ethical hacker, security consultant, expert witness, and professional speaker.

> 66 Organized criminals devise ever more ingenious attacks to steal personal information, gain intellectual property, and disrupt individual businesses and public institutions. Motivated by financial or political gain, these individuals are well funded and immensely capable. 99

—Rob Warmack, "Countering Cyber Terrorism," *Business Computing World* (blog), November 7, 2011.
www.businesscomputingworld.co.uk.

Warmack is the senior director of international marketing for Tripwire, a security software development company based in Portland, Oregon.

> 66 In addition to the individual hackers that can do damage, we have groups of activists that bring their political agendas from the physical world into the online world. These groups conduct denial of service attacks and trade in stolen information to push their message forward. 99

—Larry Clinton, testimony before the US House of Representatives' Subcommittee on Communications and Technology, February 8, 2012. http://republicans.energycommerce.house.gov.

Clinton is president and chief executive officer of the Internet Security Alliance, a coalition of Internet companies and researchers focused on Internet security matters.

Facts and Illustrations

Is Hacking Justifiable?

- Hacktivist groups accounted for **58 percent** of all the electronic data theft that occurred in 2011, according to Verizon Communications' *2012 Data Breach Investigations Report*.

- Hacktivists' volume of break-ins to the technology systems of large organizations during 2011 **exceeded** their volume of large organization break-ins in all previous years combined, according to Verizon's *2012 Data Breach Investigations Report*.

- Technology research firm Gartner predicts that financial gain, rather than advancing political ideas, will be the primary motivation for **70 percent** of the illegal hacking and other cybercrimes that occur from 2012 through 2015.

- More than **twenty-six thousand** websites in India were hacked between 2011 and early 2012, reportedly by hacktivist groups that included Anonymous and a Pakistani group called Black Hat Hackers.

- In 2011 hackers and other cybercriminals distributed **fifty-five thousand** new pieces of malware daily, or one per second, according to the Defense Department's US Cyber Command unit.

- Cisco Systems says in its *4Q 2010 Global Threat Report* that the distribution of malware increased by **139 percent** between 2009 and 2010.

Hacktivist Group Tops in *Time* 100 Voting

When *TIME* magazine polled members of the public to learn who they felt were the world's 100 most influential people in 2012, the hacktivist group Anonymous raked in the most "yes" votes. Their 395,793 votes were 131,600 more than the runner-up Erik Martin, general manager of the Internet news site Reddit and 370,420 more than President Barack Obama, who came in at number 21. In its description of the group, the magazine wrote: "United, if at all, by a taste for shock humor and disdain for authority, this leaderless Internet hive brain is plundering and playing in the electronic networks of an ever shifting enemies list: Arab dictatorships, the Vatican, banking and entertainment firms, the FBI and CIA, the security firm Stratfor and even San Francisco's BART transport system." In response to speculation that Anonymous had fixed the *TIME* 100 poll, the magazine noted, "Anonymous earned its place on the list, one way or the other."

Name	Number of "Yes" Votes
Anonymous	395,793
Erik Martin	264,193
Narendra Modi	256,792
Asghar Farhadi	140,785
Imran Khan	116,130
Alexei Navalny	92,095
Benedict Cumberbatch	91,840
Bashar Assad	91,632
Jeremy Lin	89,691
Lionel Messi	78,987
Vladimir Putin	71,584
Ron Paul	70,473
Novak Djokovic	65,117
Aung San Suu Kyi	45,688
Adele	44,180
Timothy Dolan	42,796
Cecile Richards	38,942
Lady Gaga	32,393
Shakira	30,056
Jan Brewer	26,174
Barack Obama	25,373

Source: *TIME*, "Poll Results: The 2012 *TIME* 100 Poll," 2012. www.time.com.

Eastern Europe Is Ground Zero for Hacking Attacks

The vast majority of hacking attacks in 2010 originated in Eastern European countries, including Russia and Turkey, according to a 2011 report compiled by Verizon and government agencies in the United States and Netherlands. North America ranked second as the point of origin for hacking attacks, although it lags far behind Eastern Europe. That gap, the report noted may be explained by widespread and profile hacking attacks involving organized criminal groups in Eastern Europe.

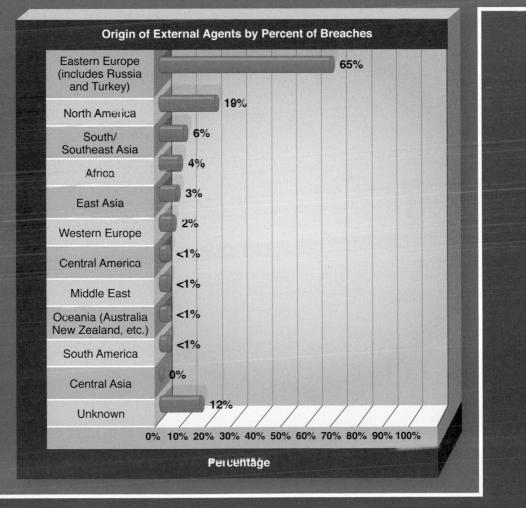

Origin of External Agents by Percent of Breaches

Region	Percentage
Eastern Europe (includes Russia and Turkey)	65%
North America	19%
South/Southeast Asia	6%
Africa	4%
East Asia	3%
Western Europe	2%
Central America	<1%
Middle East	<1%
Oceania (Australia New Zealand, etc.)	<1%
South America	<1%
Central Asia	0%
Unknown	12%

Percentage

Source: Verizon, US Secret Service, and National High Tech Crime Unit of the Netherlands Policy Agency, "2011 Data Breach Investigations Report," 2011. www.verizonbusiness.com.

- **Team Evil**, a hacktivist group opposed to military activities by Israel, defaced more than eight thousand websites between June and November 2006, sometimes leaving anti-Israeli messages on the sites, according to cybersecurity consultant Jeffrey Carr.

- Hacktivists loomed as a major threat to businesses in 2012; **61 percent** of technology and security executives surveyed in early 2012 by security firm Bit9 said that hacktivists pose the biggest threat for break-ins into their businesses' networks.

- Hackers' main motivation for hacking websites is to cause the sites to go offline, or to suffer so-called downtime, according to security firm Trustwave.

Can Hackers Be Stopped?

> **Computer crime is a burgeoning area of criminality that is difficult to investigate and prosecute.**
>
> —Richard W. Downing, deputy chief of the Justice Department's Computer Crime & Intellectual Property Section.

> **We are never going to solve the cybercrime problem. We are just trying to keep a lid on it. We don't even know how many of these activities are going on. We're only aware of a fraction of what's happening. That makes it a very hard problem to deal with.**
>
> Marc Rogers, a former cybercrime investigator in the United States and Canada.

S topping hackers poses significant challenges. Tracking down the source (or sources) of an attack is a big challenge for law enforcement and security specialists. The adoption of laws and penalties that actually deter hacking attacks is a major challenge for lawmakers. And convincing young would-be hackers that their actions can have serious consequences for real people is another.

Despite the many challenges, the FBI recorded a major victory in the battle against hacktivists in March 2012. It arrested members of Anonymous and AntiSec on charges related to breaking in to the computer system of Strategic Forecasting in December 2011. The company, also called Stratfor, gathers and analyzes intelligence on terrorism and other military-related matters and advises governments and private businesses on those issues. The hacktivist group members were charged with breaking in to the e-mail folders of Stratfor employees to steal messages that contained information on the company's inner workings and dealings with defense companies and governments. Some of those arrested were also charged with stealing Stratfor customer account information and using the information to make more than seven hundred thousand dollars' worth of unauthorized credit card purchases.

The FBI action represented one of the largest arrests made in an act linked to hacktivists. The FBI estimates the hack in this case affected about 860,000 victims, including Stratfor employees and clients. This was also one of the few arrests in which hacktivist group members were charged with theft for financial gain, namely the unauthorized credit card purchases.

Governments Expand the Hacking Fight

The United States has been a leader in efforts to halt the threat of hacking. One of the first bills, passed by Congress in 1986, was the Computer Fraud and Abuse Act. This law identified the act of gaining unauthorized access to computers as a crime. In the wake of widespread hacking attacks in 2011, the US government expanded its cybercrime efforts. The Obama administration proposed a law under which hackers would face twenty years in prison for endangering national security, 10 years for stealing data, and three years for accessing a government computer. In addition to the proposed Cybersecurity Act, other anti-hacker bills introduced in 2012 included the Cybersecurity Enhancement Act, which would fund cybersecurity research, awareness, and education. The proposed law is designed to help develop and evaluate new security technologies. Says the bill's sponsor, Senator Robert Menendez of New Jersey, "Cyber-threats are not on the horizon, they are upon us. Businesses and investors must trust that their investments are secure."[36]

Some security experts speculate that Monsegur's arrest may slow down hacktivist activity, at least for a while.

Other countries have joined the fight against hacking. Germany's cybercrime law is Europe's most forceful anti-hacking law. Its provisions include making the manufacture or possession of hacking tools a crime punishable by up to ten years in prison. Great Britain and China also have laws that make hacking a criminal offense.

FBI Recruits Hackers as Informants

The FBI has established specialized cybercrime-fighting units in all of its field offices, which have in turn helped develop new ways to fight hackers. One relatively new initiative involves recruiting hackers as informants. The recruitment efforts met success in 2011 when Hector Monsegur, a leader of LulzSec and an important member of Anonymous, became an FBI informant. Monsegur agreed to this arrangement after pleading guilty to charges related to hackings of Sony, the Public Broadcasting Service, and several other organizations. Monsegur, known online as Sabu, agreed to be an informant in exchange for a reduced sentence and is believed to have provided some of the information the FBI used for the investigation and arrests made in the Stratfor case.

Some security experts speculate that Monsegur's arrest may slow down hacktivist activity, at least for a while. "Now that Anonymous realizes [Monsegur] was a snitch and was working on his own for the Fed, they must be thinking: 'If we can't trust Sabu, who can we trust?"[37] says Mikko Hypponen, chief research officer at Finnish computer security company F-Secure.

Resistance to Cybercrime Laws

Cybercrime laws have been opposed in some countries for being too sweeping and for violating individual rights. In 2008 Germany's highest court, the Federal Constitutional Court, ruled that a provision in the country's cybercrime law allowing police to use spyware to track suspected hackers violated that country's constitution. In 2011 Germany's Chaos Computer Club group of hackers accused the country's Federal Criminal Police Office of using spyware in violation of the court ruling. The German government began an investigation in 2012.

In America some providers of e-mail services oppose a law that gives police the right to access information from e-mail accounts without first getting a search warrant. Police have used the Electronic Communications Privacy Act to obtain e-mailed messages in their investigation of Jacob Appelbaum. Appelbaum is a computer security researcher at the University of Washington who is also a self-professed hacker and part of the WikiLeaks' news distribution group. His e-mail service providers,

Google and Sonic, both unsuccessfully challenged police accessing their site without prior notification. The companies say they were concerned that allowing police to access e-mail accounts without first obtaining search warrants infringes on account holders' rights to privacy.

The Technology Industry Steps Up Its Efforts

Researchers and security experts from major technology companies and universities are joining forces to fight hacking and other cybercrime. In 2010 Microsoft, the world's largest software company, established the Microsoft Digital Crimes Unit, an international team of lawyers, investigators, technical analysts, and other specialists tasked with guarding against hackers and other cybercriminals. The group has been working with other technology companies and police worldwide in efforts that include taking down the infamous Rustock botnet in 2011. Rustock, which like other botnets used a worm to gain control of personal computers, had at one point controlled 1.6 million to 2.4 million computers. It was responsible for distributing about 30 billion e-mail spam messages daily, or more than 30 percent of the e-mail spam being distributed worldwide. After shutting down the botnet, Microsoft offered a reward of $150,000 to anyone who could provide evidence to prosecute Rustock's operators. The FBI has taken over the case, and early investigative work showed that Rustock's operators may have been using computer equipment in Russia.

> "Cybercrime laws have been opposed in some countries for being too sweeping and for violating individual rights."

The technology industry also has created a new designation of Certified Information Systems Security Professionals, or CISSPs, specially trained to bolster computer system defenses against hacking and to spot and repair areas vulnerable to hack attacks. There were eighty thousand certified CISSPs working around the world as of September 2011. The association in charge of overseeing standards for the designation, the International Information Systems Security Certification Consortium, says that in order to meet the demand for fighting hackers and other cybercriminals, at least another 2 million certified security professionals will be needed by 2014. Says the consortium's executive director, W. Hord Tipton, "I've yet to get an answer from any security professional that [their companies] had the people they needed to implement the basic security practices that are necessary to slow this [computer hacking] onslaught."[38]

Researchers and other white hat hackers are also working together to develop some distinctive weapons. They include co-called honeypots of computers that are irresistible to malicious software, particularly worms. Once they are infected by malware, the honeypot computers can lead security professionals to the hackers who originated the malware.

Businesses Take Action

To help the operators of Internet service provider companies and publicly used computer networks guard against worms and other malware distributed by hackers, the Federal Communications Commission established a new set of policies in 2012. The policies, known as the US Anti-Bot Code of Conduct, represent the first unified defense effort by those companies. The policies include steps to determine whether networks are infected, to share information with other network operators, and to educate customers on how to inspect their computers and remove malware on them.

Financial services companies, which are usually very protective of information about their operations, also began sharing information in early 2012 in an effort to fight online theft by hackers. The Wall Street firms Morgan Stanley and Goldman Sachs have partnered with the Polytechnic Institute of New York University to create a center that can sift through data from many banks to detect potential hacking attacks. "Just as the fraudsters collaborate with each other, we as an industry must collaborate,"[39] says Keith Gordon, senior vice president of security for Bank of America.

> " In order to meet the demand for fighting hackers and other cyber-criminals, at least another 2 million certified security professionals will be needed by 2014. "

While 36 percent of small and mid-sized businesses unveiled plans to boost their spending on information technology security in 2010, more than double that number said they considered data security a top priority, according to technology industry research firm Forrester Research. In most cases the businesses that ranked security high but did not budget to improve their systems simply lacked funding to do so. The National Retail Federation, a trade association for retail businesses, says that most small retail business owners want to better secure their customers' credit card data but cannot afford to do so.

And with businesses having a strong demand for certified security professionals, the salaries for those professionals will likely increase, making security against hackers even less affordable. The average salary for systems security administrators in 2011 rose 6 percent to a range of $89,000 to $121,500, according to the employment trends research company Robert Half Technology.

Hackers Cutting Through Security Software

Security software available for sale from vendors like Symantec and McAfee has proved largely successful in fending off viruses and other forms of malicious software when used properly. But many computer users do not know how to use or install it correctly. Microsoft estimates that 5 percent of computer users incorrectly handle their antivirus software and in some cases download malicious software despite warnings on their computer screens advising them not to do so.

Meanwhile, individual personal computer owners looking to protect their systems but also to save money will sometimes use inferior antivirus software that is offered for free. Antivirus software that is paid for captured 49 percent more malicious software than free software captured in a test conducted by *PCWorld* magazine.

Hackers Moving Faster than Defenders

If the white hats are ever to stop the black hat hackers, they are going to have to speed things up. A study by consulting firm Deloitte finds that the malicious hackers are developing new attack methods more rapidly than their victims can counter with defenses. Technology industry analysts warn that a new wave of "advanced persistent threat" attacks may be insurmountable for many companies. Those advanced attacks typically include a series of assaults that use different techniques to probe defense systems until finding one that can be bypassed.

Advanced persistent threat attack victims in 2011 included the internationally known Internet security firm RSA. Hackers broke in to and compromised the American company's security system. That system is used by clients that include several global telecommunications companies and Lockheed Martin, a major US defense contractor. Hacking attacks like this one add to the growing sense that all companies, even those with advanced technology security systems, will have to take more expensive steps to protect themselves from hackers. Even then, some wonder if this will be enough. "The threat vectors we've seen have changed drastically. Compromise is inevitable, data loss is inevitable, what do we do?"[40] asks Perry Olson, a senior director for computer chip maker Intel.

> **Because hacking occurs on a global scale, security experts say that international cooperation is essential to stopping hacker attacks.**

International Cooperation Is Needed

Because hacking occurs on a global scale, security experts say that international cooperation is essential to stopping hacker attacks. For instance, New York investigators worked with police in Europe, Asia, and Africa on a case involving an Africa-based crime ring that had targeted the credit cards of US consumers. Members of the crime ring were arrested in New York in October 2011 after using stolen credit card numbers to make $13 million worth of illegal purchases. According to law enforcement officials, members of the ring inserted devices into credit card processing machines at stores and restaurants in New York City and Long Island, New York. The devices lifted the stored credit card information, which was then used to make duplicate credit cards. Says Robert Siciliano, an identity theft expert, "Despite bad blood between countries and their politics, when it comes to fraud regarding economic systems, governments and their security forces are coming together like never before."[41]

Police and government investigators have been recording major victories in their fight against malicious hackers. But the black hats continue to devise new strategies and weapons, setting the stage for ongoing and costly battles.

Primary Source Quotes*

Can Hackers Be Stopped?

66 **Threats posed to organizations by cybercrimes have increased faster than potential victims—or cyber security professionals—can cope with them, placing targeted organizations at significant risk.** 99

—Deloitte, *Cyber Crime: A Clear and Present Danger; Combating the Fastest Growing Cyber Security Threat*. New York: Deloitte, 2010.

Deloitte is an international business services and consulting firm.

66 **While cyber-criminals operate in a world without borders, the law enforcement community does not. The increasingly multi-national, multi-jurisdictional nature of cybercrime cases has increased the time and resources needed for successful investigation and adjudication.** 99

—Pablo A. Martinez, testimony before the US Senate Committee on the Judiciary, Subcommittee on Crime and Terrorism, September 9, 2011. www.dhs.gov.

Martinez is the US Secret Service deputy special agent in charge of the agency's criminal investigative division.

* Editor's Note: While the definition of a primary source can be narrowly or broadly defined, for the purposes of Compact Research, a primary source consists of: 1) results of original research presented by an organization or researcher; 2) eyewitness accounts of events, personal experience, or work experience; 3) first-person editorials offering pundits' opinions; 4) government officials presenting political plans and/or policies; 5) representatives of organizations presenting testimony or policy.

❝There is no longer anything unusual about malware attacks and data breaches. Most happen in everyday circumstances, and classic anti-virus software is designed to block just some of the threats.❞

—John Metzger and Jonathan Shaw, "Eight Threats Your Anti-virus Won't Stop: Why You Need Endpoint Security," White Paper, Sophos, 2010.

Metzger is senior product marketing manager and Jonathan Shaw a product manager for Sophos, a technology security software developer with main offices in Boston and Oxford, England.

❝In order to address the rising number and in some cases the sophistication of cyber attacks, IDC believes that organizations will need to approach security in a different way. The traditional methods of isolating systems through firewalls will not be sufficient as the systems become more complex.❞

—Matt Healey, "Thoughts on the Increase in Cyber Attacks," *IDC Circle Blogs*, October 5, 2011. www.idccircle.com.

Healey is program director of software and services in the Asia-Pacific region for IDC, a technology research and advisory firm in Framingham, Massachusetts.

❝Security isn't a standalone function, but one that must be integrated into all aspects of the information system.❞

—John Sankovich, "Cybersecurity: A Continuous Monitoring Action Plan," *Information Week* February 2011.

Sankovich is the head of the government health-care technology practice at Truestone, an information security services company in Herndon, Virgina.

66 So how do you protect your network from trojans? A common misconception is that antivirus software offers all the protection you need. The truth is antivirus software offers only limited protection.99

—GFI Software, "The Corporate Threat Posed by Email Trojans: How to Protect Your Network Against Trojans," White Paper, GFI Software, 2011.

GFI Software is a developer of security software for small and medium-sized businesses and has offices in America, Europe, Asia, and Australia.

66 Targeted attacks are penetrating standard levels of security controls and causing significant business damage to enterprises that do not evolve their security controls.99

—John Pescatore, in "Gartner Highlights Strategies for Dealing with the Increase in Advanced Targeted Threats," press release, Gartner, August 24, 2011. www.gartner.com.

Pescatore is an analyst at and the vice president of technology research company Gartner.

66 Defence against cyberweapons has to concentrate on resilience—preventative measures plus detailed contingency plans to enable rapid recovery when an attack succeeds.99

—Peter Sommer and Ian Brown, *Reducing Systemic Cybersecurity Risk*, OECD/IFP Project on Future Global Shocks, January 14, 2011. www.oecd.org.

Sommer is with the Information Systems and Innovation Group of London School of Economics; Brown is with the Oxford Internet Institute of Oxford University.

Facts and Illustrations

Can Hackers Be Stopped?

- Only about **25 percent** of the electronic data stored by business and government organizations is properly protected, says International Data Corporation's 2011 report, *Effective Data Leak Prevention Programs: Start by Protecting Data at the Source—Your Databases.*

- **Forty percent** of business leaders surveyed in seventy eight countries said their organizations do not have the capability to detect and prevent cybercrime, according to a 2011 survey conducted by the consulting firm PricewaterhouseCoopers.

- About **25 percent** of the hackers in America have been recruited by the FBI and other law enforcement officials to help fight illegal hacking, according to Eric Corley, publisher of the hacker newsletter *2600.*

- **Seventy-two percent** of small businesses in America do not have a formal policy for Internet security, according to a 2011 report by the Better Business Bureau.

- Only **59 percent** of chief technology officers at large businesses worldwide said they were very confident of their organization's ability to fend off a hacking attack, according to a 2011 survey by *Computerworld magazine.*

- In an indication that defenses against **botnets** may be succeeding, the average number of computers that botnets infected and operated from shrank to **twenty thousand** in 2011 from a high of one hundred thousand in 2004, says F5, a technology security firm in Seattle, Washington.

Barriers to Information Security at Financial Institutions

Banks and other financial institutions have experienced significant challenges in stopping hacking attacks. When asked to identify the top barriers to ensuring secure electronic data at their institutions, nearly 20 percent of respondents cited a lack of budget. Increasing sophistication of hacking attacks was cited as one of the top three barriers.

Question:

What are the Top 2 Barriers You Face in Ensuring Information Security?

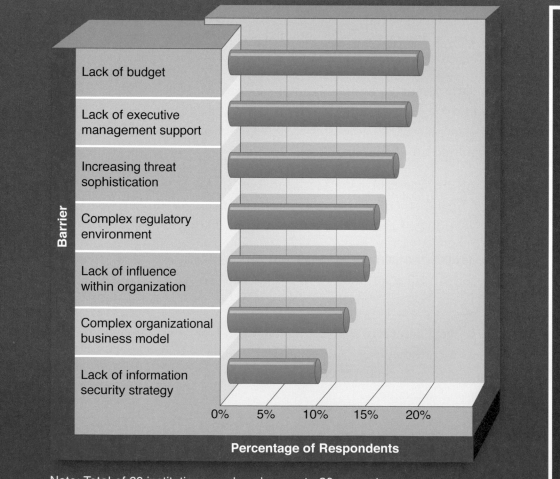

Note: Total of 60 institutions; scale only goes to 20 percent.

Percentage of Respondents

Source: International Data Corp./IDC Financial Insights, "New Threats Demand Innovative Responses," 2011. www.infosec.co.uk.

Preparation for Hacking Attacks Is Mixed

A majority of businesses worldwide say they are somewhat or extremely prepared for malware attacks, according to a 2011 survey by security software company McAfee. About half as many say they are as prepared to fend off a distributed denial of service (DDOS) attack, in which hackers use botnets to bombard computer networks or websites with so much data that they shut down.

How Prepared Are Companies?

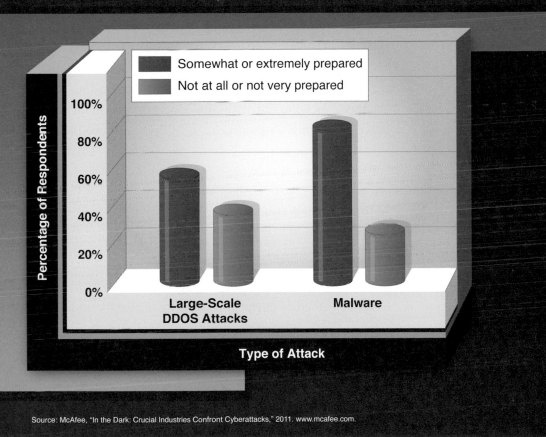

Source: McAfee, "In the Dark: Crucial Industries Confront Cyberattacks," 2011. www.mcafee.com.

- The average starting salary for data security analysts in 2011 rose **6 percent** to a range of $89,000 to $121,500. That was the second-highest salary increase among all technology industry positions, according to employment services firm Robert Half Technology.

Key People and Advocacy Groups

Julian Assange: The editor in chief and founder of WikiLeaks, an Internet-based publisher, is widely considered a hacktivist because WikiLeaks publishes classified government documents that are sometimes obtained by hackers. He was a self-proclaimed hacker in his home country of Australia before becoming known as an activist who traveled the world to make public appearances on behalf of causes that included freedom of the press.

Steve Ballmer: The chief executive officer of Microsoft, who became the company's leader after Bill Gates retired in 2008, has a lot riding on the fight against hackers. The company's Windows operating systems are the platforms in place in roughly 75 percent of all computers and networks worldwide. So hackers, such as those behind the Conficker worm, have targeted vulnerabilities in the Windows systems in order to penetrate millions of computers with one hack. Under Ballmer, Microsoft has been one of the major forces in the fight against cybercrime.

Richard A. Clarke: A former member of America's National Security Council under presidents George H.W. Bush, Bill Clinton, and George W. Bush, he is the most vocal critic of the cybersecurity initiatives undertaken by President Barack Obama. He has warned that the policies are too lax in his public appearances, newspaper columns, and the book *Cyber War: The Next Threat to National Security and What to Do About It*, published in 2010.

Shawn Henry: In the time since he was appointed executive assistant director of the FBI's Criminal, Cyber, Response, and Services Branch in September 2010, the unit has made arrests in the biggest cybercrime cases in the FBI's history. These include the 2011 arrest of a ring charged with the theft and subsequent reselling of more than 170 million credit and debit cards from victims that included TJX Companies, and the 2012 arrest of several prominent members of the LulzSec and Anonymous hacktivist groups.

Kevin Mitnick: The information security consultant has become a hacker celebrity known worldwide because he was once the most wanted malicious hacker, sought by police for breaking in to the systems of prominent government agencies and businesses in America. After serving time in prison and then becoming a security specialist, he emerged as an international authority on hacking, testified before the US Congress, was the subject of the 2000 movie *Takedown*, appeared on television talk shows, and wrote books about his exploits.

Hector "Sabu" Monsegur: The co-leader of LulzSec, who was arrested in 2011 and became an FBI informant, could help investors make more hacking arrests depending on how much information he provides.

Jeff Moss: America's most prominent white hat hacker, he is part of the Homeland Security Advisory Council. which advises the president on national security issues, and is also chief security officer of the Internet Corporation for Assigned Names and Numbers, which oversees major aspects of the Internet's security. He also cofounded and manages the world's two largest annual conventions for hackers, DEF CON and Black Hat.

Janet Napolitano: The secretary of the Homeland Security Department is also the ultimate boss of the department's National Cyber Security Division. That unit was created to build a national cyberspace response system and to establish a program that protects America's infrastructure from cyberattacks.

Leon Panetta: As America's secretary of defense, Panetta is positioned to further intensify the military's focus on defending against hackers and other cybercriminals. During his tenure as director of the CIA from February 2009 to April 2011, that agency made investing in technology to fight cyberthreats one of its three main priorities.

Chronology

1932
In what is considered the first computer hacking act, a team of Polish mathematicians, led by Marian Rejewski, break the code for the Enigma messaging machine used by Nazi Germany's military.

1969
The Internet's framework is established when the first communication is sent across the Advanced Research Projects Agency Network (ARPANET), a program funded by the Defense Department that enables computers to exchange data with each other.

1986
The US Computer Fraud and Abuse Act becomes law, establishing unauthorized access of a computer as a criminal act subject to stiff penalties that include prison terms.

1981
The world's first hacktivist group, the Chaos Computer Club, organizes in Germany. Three years later it hacks its home country's postal service system.

1930

1960

1980

1971
E-mail is invented and put to work by the users of ARPANET.

1982
A group of Wisconsin youths, known as the 414s, hack the computer systems of more than fifty major organizations that include the Los Alamos National Laboratory in New Mexico and the Memorial Sloan-Kettering Cancer Center in New York.

1984
In an indication of hacking's growing international fame, the Chaos Computer Club holds its first annual hacking convention in Hamburg, Germany.

1958
The term *hacker* becomes popularly associated with computers when it is used by members of the Tech Model Railroad Club at the Massachusetts Institute of Technology, a group that finds ways to obtain unauthorized access to the university's mainframe computer.

1973
Computer security becomes a national concern as individuals begin to break in to telephone systems, in some cases to make long-distance calls for free, an act known as "phreaking."

1983
Hollywood releases the first hacking movie, *War Games*, about a boy who unwittingly hacks into the Defense Department's nuclear combat simulator computer.

1988

Robert T. Morris creates and releases the first malware worm to be spread over the ARPANET. He also becomes the first person convicted under the 1986 Computer Fraud and Abuse Act.

2008

Shortly after he wins the US presidential election, Barack Obama is advised that the United States is at risk of sustaining major damage from a cyberattack. After taking office, he identifies cybersecurity as a major issue for his administration.

2011

Hacktivist groups Anonymous and LulzSec take credit for a wave of hacking attacks on private businesses and state and federal government agencies, including the CIA and the FBI.

1998

Ehud Tenenbaum, an Israeli hacker known as "The Analyzer," hacks Defense Department computers and steals software programs.

2006

In one of the largest-scale hacking attacks to date, hackers from eastern Europe and America breach the systems of retail store chain company TJX Companies to steal the credit and debit card numbers of 40 million of its customers.

1990

2010

1995

Kevin Mitnick is arrested for hackings that cost software companies millions of dollars in lost sales. Five years later, he testifies at a US congressional hearing regarding the need for stricter cybersecurity laws.

2007

Russia launches a cyberattack on its neighbor Estonia, crippling the country's Internet communications.

2009

A hacking attack launched by North Korea knocks out the website servers of the US Treasury, Secret Service, Federal Trade Commission, and Department of Transportation.

1999

Russian hackers take $10 million from Citibank and transfer the money to bank accounts around the world. The ringleader, Vladimir Levin, is convicted in the United States, sentenced to three years in prison, and ordered to pay restitution. Citibank recovers all but four hundred thousand dollars of the stolen money.

2012

The FBI announces the arrest of five members of the LulzSec, Anonymous, and AntiSec hacktivist groups. Those arrested include one of LulzSec's leaders, Hector Monsegur.

Related Organizations

Computer Security Resource Center (CSRC)

National Institute of Standards and Technology
100 Bureau Dr., Stop 1070
Gaithersburg, MD 20899-1070
phone: (301) 975-6478
website: http://csrc.nist.gov

The CSRC researches computer security technologies and establishes guidelines and standards for businesses and government agencies to follow in their use of those technologies. The center is part of the National Institute of Standards and Technology, which is a group within the US Department of Commerce.

Cyber Security Research & Development Center (CSRDC)

c/o SRI International
333 Ravenswood Ave.
Menlo Park, CA 94025
phone: (650) 859-2000
website: www.cyber.st.dhs.gov

The CSRDC was established by the Homeland Security Department in 2004 to develop security technology for the protection of America's key infrastructure areas. It conducts its work through relationships with other government agencies, private businesses, and research organizations.

Electronic Privacy Information Center (EPIC)

1718 Connecticut Ave. NW, #200
Washington, DC 20009
(202) 483-1140
website: www.epic.org

EPIC is a public interest research organization focused on public issues that relate to technology, particularly the privacy of citizens. Its members testify before the US Congress and files motions in the courts on behalf of consumers.

Identity Theft Resource Center (ITRC)

9672 Via Excelencia, #101
San Diego, CA 92126
phone: (858) 693-7935
website: www.idtheftcenter.org

This organization researches thefts of identifying information such as Social Security numbers and driver's license numbers and pulls its information together to make the public aware of the extent of these thefts. It also seeks to educate consumers and businesses on how to guard against becoming victims.

International Information Systems Security Certification Consortium (ISC)

1964 Gallows Rd., Suite 210
Vienna, VA 22182
phone: (866) 462-4777 • fax: (703) 356-7977
website: www.isc2.org

This is a nonprofit organization that oversees the training of technology security workers and administers the Certified Information Systems Security Professional certification program for those workers. It publishes a monthly magazine that reports on major trends and issues in cybersecurity.

International Multilateral Partnership Against Cyber Threats (IMPACT)

63000 Cyberjaya
Malaysia
phone: 60 (3) 8313 2020
website: www.impact-alliance.org

This group is an arm of the United Nations. It brings together governments and technology experts from around the world to develop strategies and techniques for combating hacking and other threats to computerized operations. It has 193 member countries.

Microsoft Digital Crimes Unit

Microsoft Corporation
One Microsoft Way
Redmond, WA 98052-6399
phone: (800) 285-7772 • fax: (425) 706-7329
website: www.msft@microsoft.com

The Microsoft Digital Crimes Unit is an international team of lawyers, investigators, technical analysts, and other specialists who collaborate to protect technology systems from hackers and other forms of cybercrime and to investigate computer system break-ins. The unit also alerts the public about existing or looming threats on the Internet.

Shadowserver Foundation

www.shadowserver.org

The Shadowserver Foundation is a nonprofit, all-volunteer watchdog group of security professionals that tracks and reports information on malware, botnet activity, and electronic fraud. It seeks to raise the public's awareness of Internet threats.

US Department of Justice

Computer Crime & Intellectual Property Section
Tenth and Constitution Ave. NW
John C. Keeney Building, Suite 600
Washington, DC 20530
phone: (202) 514-2007
website: www.cybercrime.gov

This agency is responsible for carrying out the Justice Department's strategies for combating computer crimes worldwide. It works with other government agencies, businesses, colleges, universities, other nongovernmental groups, and foreign countries to prevent, investigate, and prosecute computer crime cases.

WikiLeaks

University of Melbourne
PO Box 4080
Victoria 3052
Australia
www.wikileaks.org

WikiLeaks is a not-for-profit media organization whose published materials have included documents hacked from the technology systems of government organizations worldwide. Its website includes links to news stories about its activities and the controversies in which it has a major role.

For Further Research

Books

Mark Bowden, *Worm: The First Digital World War*. New York: *Atlantic Monthly* Press, 2011.

Michael Calce, *Mafiaboy: A Portrait of the Hacker as a Young Man*. Guilford, CT: Lyons, 2011.

Jeffrey Carr, *Inside Cyber Warfare*. Sebastopol, CA: O'Reilly Media, 2010.

Richard A. Clarke and Robert K. Knake, *Cyber War: The Next Threat to National Security and What to Do About It*. New York: HarperCollins, 2010.

Steven Levy, *Hackers: Heroes of the Computer Revolution*. Sebastopol, CA: O'Reilly Media, 2010.

Kevin Mitnick with William L. Simon, *Ghost in the Wires: My Adventures as the World's Most Wanted Hacker*. New York: Little, Brown, 2011.

Richard Stiennon, *Surviving Cyber War*. Lanham, MD: Government Institutes, 2010.

Nancy Willard, *Cyber Savvy: Embracing Digital Safety and Civility*. Los Angeles: Sage, 2012.

Periodicals

Mark Bowden, "The Enemy Within," *Atlantic Monthly*, June 2010.

Jeffrey Brito, "Veteran Hacker Hired to Keep an Eye on Every Internet Address," *Time*, April 29, 2011.

Charlie Burton, "25 Big Ideas for 2012: Drone Hacking," *Wired*, January 2012.

Joe Dysart, "The Hacktivists: Web Vigilantes Net Attention, Outrage and Access to Your Data," *ABA Journal*, December 2011.

Michael Joseph Gross, "Enter the Cyber-dragon," *Vanity Fair*, September 2011.

Eben Harrell, "WikiLeaks' Julian Assange: The Wizard from Oz," *Time*, August 9, 2010.

Dan Kaplan, "The Legacy of LulzSec," *SC Magazine*, June 20, 2011.

David M. Nicol, "Hacking the Lights Out: The Computer Virus Threat to the Electrical Grid Computer," *Scientific American*, July 2011.

Matt Peckham, "Iranian Government Accused in Serious Net Attack," *Time*, March 24, 2011.

———, "Sony and PS3 Hacker George Hotz Kiss and Make Up," *PC-World*, April 11, 2011.

Bill Saporito, "Hack Attack," *Time*, June 23, 2011.

James Verini, "The Great Cyberheist," *New York Times Magazine*, November 2010.

Martyn Williams, "PlayStation Network Hack Timeline," *PCWorld*, May 1, 2011.

Michael Wolff, "Rupert Murdoch Blown Wide Open," *British GQ*, November 2011.

Internet Sources
ABC News, "Top 5 Famous Computer Hackers: From Conficker to the First Computer Virus," April 2, 2009. http://abcnews.go.com/Technology/story?id=7230601&page=1.

Focus, "Top 10 Most Famous Hackers of All Time," 2012. www.focus.com/fyi/top-10-most famous-hackers-all-time.

National Journal, "Analysts Say Online 'Hacktivism' Is Becoming a Preferred Tool of Protests," August 25, 2011. http://mobile.nationaljournal.com/tech/analysts-say-online-hacktivism-is-becoming-a-preferred-tool-of-protests-20110825.

PBS NewsHour, "Black Hat and Defcon Founder Jeff Moss: What Is the 'Hacker Mindset'?," August 10, 2010. www.pbs.org/newshour/rundown/2010/08/black-hat-and-defcon-founder-jeff-moss-what-is-the-hacker-mindset.html.

SC Magazine, "Video: Hacktivism, Anonymous and the New Security Model," February 24, 2012. www.scmagazine.com/video-hacktivism-anonymous-and-the-new-security-model/article/229392.

Time, "WikiLeaks Founder Julian Assange," July 26, 2010. www.time.com/time/world/article/0,8599,2006496,00.html#ixzz1omROucYZ.

Source Notes

Overview

1. Steven R. Chabinsky, GovSec Government Security Conference & Expo, Washington, DC, March 23, 2010.
2. Brian Harvey, "What Is a Hacker?," Electrical Engineering and Computer Sciences Division, University of California–Berkeley. www.cs.berkeley.edu.
3. Dave DeWalt, *Unsecured Economies: Protecting Vital Information*. Santa Clara, CA: McAfee, 2011, p. 1.
4. Quoted in CNN, "Twitter Hackers Appear to Be Shiite Group," CNN.com, Dec, 18, 2009. http://articles.cnn.com.
5. Quoted in Jeremy Kirk, "Raytheon's Cyberchief Describes 'Come to Jesus' Moment," *Computerworld*, October 12, 2011. www.computerworld.com.
6. Quoted in *Daily Mail Reporter* "Hacked! First the Senate, Now the CIA: Computer Gang Accesses Agency Website to Help Government Fix Their Issues," June 16, 2011, www.dailymail.co.uk.
7. Secure Computing Corporation, *What E-mail Hackers Know That You Don't*. San Jose, CA: Secure Computing Corporation, 2011, p. 1.

How Serious Is the Threat from Hacking?

8. Martin Lee, *Calculating the Costs: Email Threats & Financial Risks*. New York: Symantec.cloud, 2011, p. 2.
9. Quoted in FBI, "Manhattan U.S. Attorney Charges Seven Individuals for Engineering Sophisticated Internet Fraud Scheme That Infected Millions of Computers Worldwide and Manip-
ulated Internet Advertising Business," press release, November 9, 2011. www.fbi.gov.
10. Richard Stiennon, *Surviving Cyber War*. Lanham, MD: Government Institutes, 2010, p. 55.
11. Kevin Beaver, *Hacking for Dummies*, 3rd ed. Hoboken, NJ: Wiley, 2010, p. 27.

Does Hacking Threaten National Security?

12. Quoted in U.S. Senate Committee on Armed Services, "Hearing to Consider the Nomination of Hon. Leon E. Panetta to Be Secretary of Defense," transcript, June 9, 2011. http://armed-services.senate.gov.
13. Mike McConnell, Michael Chertoff, and William Lynn, "China's Cyber Thievery Is National Policy—and Must Be Challenged," *Wall Street Journal*, January 27, 2012. http://online.wsj.com.
14. US–China Economic and Security Review Commission, *2011 Report to Congress*. Washington, DC: Government Printing Office, November 2011. www.uscc.gov.
15. Quoted in Michael S. Schmidt, "F.B.I. Director Warns Congress About Terrorist Hacking," *New York Times*, March 8, 2012, p. A6.
16. US–China Economic and Security Review Commission, *2011 Report to Congress*.
17. Quoted in Kim Zetter, "Google Hack Attack Was Ultra Sophisticated, New Details Show," *Wired*, January 14, 2010. www.wired.com.
18. Quoted in Eric Engleman and Chris

Strohm, "Cybersecurity Disaster Seen in U.S. Survey Citing Spending Gaps," *Bloomberg*, January 31, 2012. www.bloomberg.com.

19. Quoted in Andrea Shalal-Esa and Jim Finkle, "Exclusive: NSA Helps Banks Battle Hackers," Reuters, October 26, 2011. www.reuters.com.

20. Mike McConnell, "Mike McConnell on How to Win the Cyber-war We're Losing," *Washington Post*, February 28, 2010. www.washingtonpost.com.

21. Richard A. Clarke, "China's Cyberassault on America," *Wall Street Journal*, June 15, 2011. http://online.wsj.com.

22. Quoted in Josh Smith, "Groups Warn of Privacy Concerns in Cybersecurity Bill," *National Journal*, February 9, 2012. www.nationaljournal.com.

23. Quoted in Ellen Nakashima and David S. Hilzenrath, "Cybersecurity: SEC Outlines Requirement That Companies Report Cyber Theft and Attack," *Washington Post*, October 14, 2011. www.washingtonpost.com.

24. Symantec, *"CyberTerrorism?,"* Symantec Security Response (White Paper), 2011, p.24. www.symantec.com.

25. Government Accountability Office, *Information Security Weaknesses Continue Amid New Federal Efforts to Implement Requirements*. Washington, DC: Government Accountability Office, October 2011. www.gao.gov.

Is Hacking Justifiable?

26. George Hotz, "Graf_chokolo," *GeoHot Got Sued* (blog), February 1, 2011. http://geohotgotsued.blogspot.com.

27. Verizon Communications, *2012 Data Breach Investigations Report*. New York: Verizon Communications, 2012. www.verizonbusiness.com.

28. LulzSecurity, "Operation Anti-security," press release, Pastebin.com, June 19, 2011. http://pastebin.com.

29. Quoted in Haytham al-Tabaei, "Syrian 'Electronic Army' Confronts Revolution Online," *Asharq Alawsat*, July 7, 2011. www.asharq-e.com.

30. Lulz Security, "LulzSec—1000th Tweet Statement," press release, June 17, 2011. http://pastebin.com.

31. Peter Ludlow, "WikiLeaks and Hacktivist Culture," History News Network, George Mason University, September 20, 2010. http://hnn.us.

32. Quoted in Julian E. Barnes, Miguel Bustillo, and Christopher Rhoads, "Computer Evidence Ties Leaks to Soldier," *Wall Street Journal*, July 30, 2010. http://online.wsj.com.

33. Paul McMullan, "McMullan Justifies Phone Hacking," *Reliable Sources* (blog), CNN, July 24, 2011. http://reliablesources.blogs.cnn.com.

34. Paul Connolly, "No Justification for Phone Hacking Under Any Guise," *Belfast Telegraph*, January 10, 2011. www.belfasttelegraph.co.uk.

35. Eric Sterner, "Hacktivists' Evolution Changes Cyber Security Threat Environment," *World Politics Review*, April 23, 2012. www.worldpoliticsreview.com.

Can Hackers Be Stopped?

36. Quoted in Kevin Drawbaugh and Diane Bartz, "Anti-computer Hacking Bill Coming in Congress," *International Business Times*, February 19, 2012. www.ibtimes.com.

37. Quoted in Basil Katz and Grant McCool, "Hacking 'Mole' Helps FBI Arrest Anonymous Leaders," Thomson Reuters, March 7, 2012. http://newsandinsight.thomsonreuters.com.

38. Quoted in Eric B. Parizo, "(ISC)2 at a Crossroads: CISSP Value vs. Security Industry Growth," *Information Security*, September 23, 2011. http://

searchsecurity.techtarget.com.

39. Quoted in Suzanne Kapner, "Banks Unite to Battle Online Theft," *Wall Street Journal*, January 10, 2012. http://online.wsj.com.

40. Quoted in Jack Clark, "Intel: Data Loss from Cyberattacks Is Inevitable," *ZDNet UK*, September 13, 2011. www .zdnet.co.uk.

41. Quoted in Tracy Kitten, "Biggest ID Theft in History," Government Information Security, October 10, 2011. www.govinfosecurity.com.

List of Illustrations

How Serious Is the Threat from Hacking?

Does Hacking Threaten National Security?

Is Hacking Justifiable?

Can Hackers Be Stopped?

Index

Index

About the Author

John Covaleski, who has worked as a reporter and editor at several daily newspapers and business publications on the east coast, is on the editorial staff of *Commercial Real Estate Direct*, an investment news and research publication in Bucks County, Pennsylvania, and he does freelance writing from his suburban Philadelphia home.